HUMAN BODY Q&A

Written by Richard Walker

LONDON, NEW YORK,
MELBOURNE, MUNICH, AND DELHI

Senior Art Editor Smiljka Surla
Designer Hoa Luc
Senior Editor Fran Jones
Project Editor Niki Foreman
Additional Designers Sheila Collins, Spencer Holbrook,
Stefan Podhorodecki, Marilou Prokopiou, Jacqui Swan
Editorial Assistant Ashwin Khurana
Managing Editor Linda Esposito
Managing Art Editor Diane Thistlethwaite
Publishing Manager Andrew Macintyre
Category Publisher Laura Buller
Design Development Manager Sophia M. Tampakopoulos
Production Controller Poppy Newdick
Production Editor Melissa Latorre
DK Picture Library Ria Jones
Jacket Editor Mariza O'Keeffe
Jacket Designer Laura Brim

First published in the United States in 2010
by DK Publishing,
375 Hudson Street, New York, New York 10014

A Penguin Company
Copyright © 2010 Dorling Kindersley Limited

09 10 11 12 13 10 9 8 7 6 5 4 3 2 1
HD171 – 11/09

DK books are available at special discounts when purchased in bulk for
sales promotions, premiums, fundraising, or educational use. For details, contact:
DK Publishing Special Markets, 375 Hudson Street, New York, New York 10014
SpecialSales@dk.com

A catalog record for this book is
available from the Library of Congress.

ISBN 978-0-7566-5752-9

Printed and bound in China by Toppan
See our complete catalog at
www.dk.com

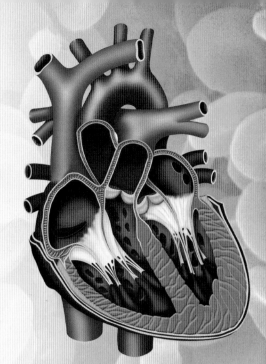

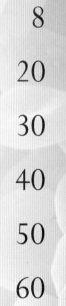

CONTENTS

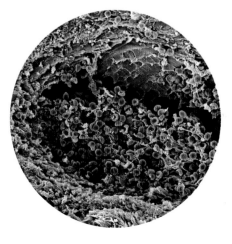

BODY PARTS

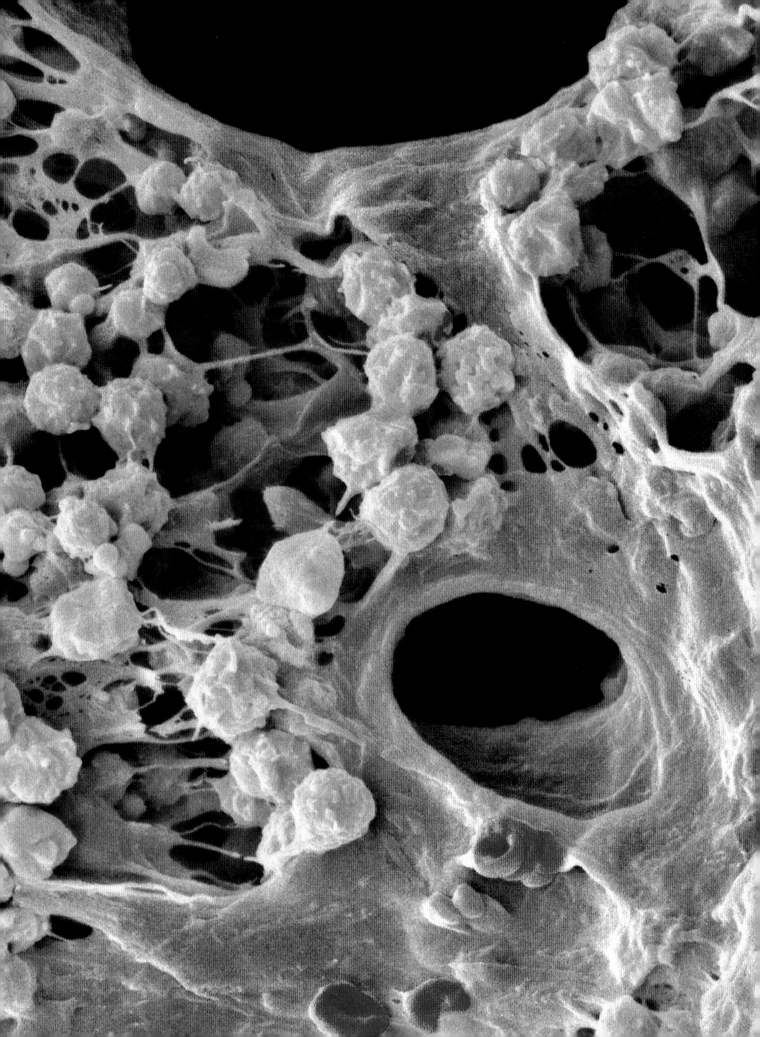

What is my body made from?

It takes about 100 trillion (100,000,000,000,000) microscopic living units called cells to make a human body. There are many different types of cells, and these are organized into the tissues and organs that make up your major body systems. These include the skeletal and muscular systems, which support and move the body, and the digestive and respiratory systems, which supply food and oxygen.

MRI scan showing body organs

Circulatory system

Heart pumps blood

Blood vessel carries blood

Q A Which is my biggest organ?

Your organs come in many shapes and sizes and perform many different roles. Your organs include skin— your body's biggest organ— the liver, which controls blood composition, the lungs, and the kidneys. Each organ has specific tasks.

The liver—the body's second-biggest organ

Q A How does my body work?

At the simplest level, cells of the same type work together in groups to form tissues. Different tissues cooperate to make organs, such as the heart, and linked organs work together to form one of the body's 12 systems. In the circulatory system, for example, the heart and blood vessels work together to carry blood all around the body.

Lung takes in oxygen

Bladder stores urine produced by the kidneys

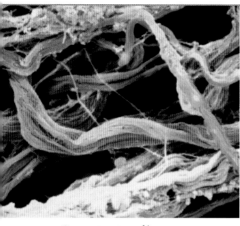
Connective tissue fibers

Q A What holds my body together?

There are four basic types of tissues in your body—epithelial, nervous, muscular, and connective. Epithelial tissues are protective; they cover the skin and line the mouth, stomach, and other organs. Nervous tissues form your body's control system—the brain and nervous system. Muscular tissues form the muscles that move you. And connective tissues, as their name suggests, hold together other tissues and your entire body.

- Bone supports the upper arm
- Kidney
- Muscle moves the fingers

Q A Are cells alive?

Although they are microscopic, cells have a complex structure. A membrane surrounds the cell and controls what enters and leaves it. Tiny structures, called organelles, float and move in the jellylike cytoplasm. Organelles each have their own jobs, but they work together to make the cell a living unit. For example, mitochondria release energy in order to power the cell's activities, while the nucleus contains the cell's operating instructions.

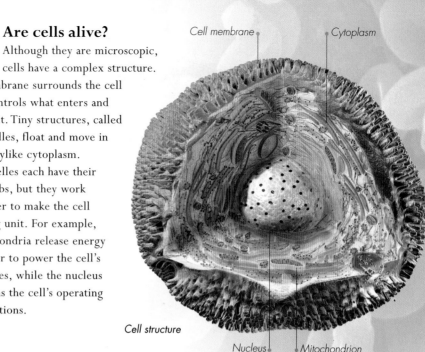
Cell membrane · Cytoplasm
Cell structure
Nucleus · Mitochondrion

Cell division

New "daughter" cell

Q A How do cells multiply?

Right now, some of your cells are dividing by a process called mitosis. Highly organized and precisely timed, mitosis enables your cells to multiply so that you can grow, maintain yourself, and replace worn-out cells. During mitosis, the instructions inside the nucleus, which are needed in order to build and run a cell, are copied and separated into two equal packages. Then the "parent" cell divides into two identical "daughter" cells, each with its own complete set of instructions.

Stem cell

More Facts

- There are more than 200 different types of cells in the body, including red blood cells, nerve cells, fat cells, and muscle cells.

- A cell lining the small intestine has a life span of just 36 hours, while a red blood cell lives for four months, and a brain cell can last a lifetime.

- An egg, or ovum, released from a woman's ovary, is at least 0.0039 in (0.1 mm) across and is the biggest cell in the body.

- Stem cells are found in various body tissues. They multiply rapidly to produce cells that become specialized to do a specific job. In red bone marrow, for example, stem cells produce blood cells

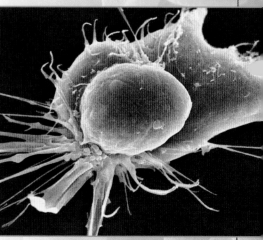

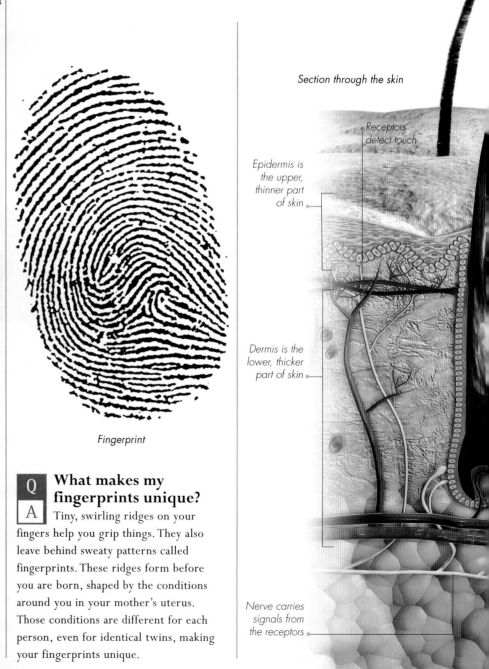

Is skin alive?

Enclosing your body like a winter coat, skin is a tough, waterproof, germ-proof barrier that separates your insides from the harsh outside world. It also houses receptors that detect touch, pressure, heat, cold, and pain. The skin has two parts: the epidermis and the dermis. The protective epidermis constantly produces cells that migrate upward to the skin's surface where they flatten, die, and are worn away as skin flakes. Very much alive, the lower dermis contains blood vessels, hair follicles, sweat glands, and sensory receptors.

Melanocytes in the epidermis

Q / A What makes skin the color it is?

Deep in the epidermis, cells called melanocytes release melanin—a brown pigment that colours your skin. Melanin also filters out harmful ultraviolet radiation in sunlight that can damage skin cells. We all have the same number of melanocytes, but they produce more melanin in people with darker skin.

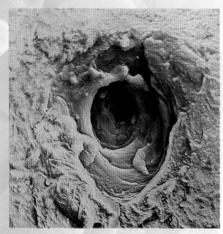

Sweat pore

Q / A Why do I sweat when it's hot?

Your skin helps keep your body temperature at a steady 98.6°F (37°C). If it's hot, sweat released onto your skin's surface evaporates and cools you down. At the same time, blood vessels near the skin's surface widen and release heat. If it's cold, you stop sweating and the blood vessels narrow to cut heat loss.

Fingerprint

Q / A What makes my fingerprints unique?

Tiny, swirling ridges on your fingers help you grip things. They also leave behind sweaty patterns called fingerprints. These ridges form before you are born, shaped by the conditions around you in your mother's uterus. Those conditions are different for each person, even for identical twins, making your fingerprints unique.

Section through the skin

Receptors detect touch

Epidermis is the upper, thinner part of skin

Dermis is the lower, thicker part of skin

Nerve carries signals from the receptors

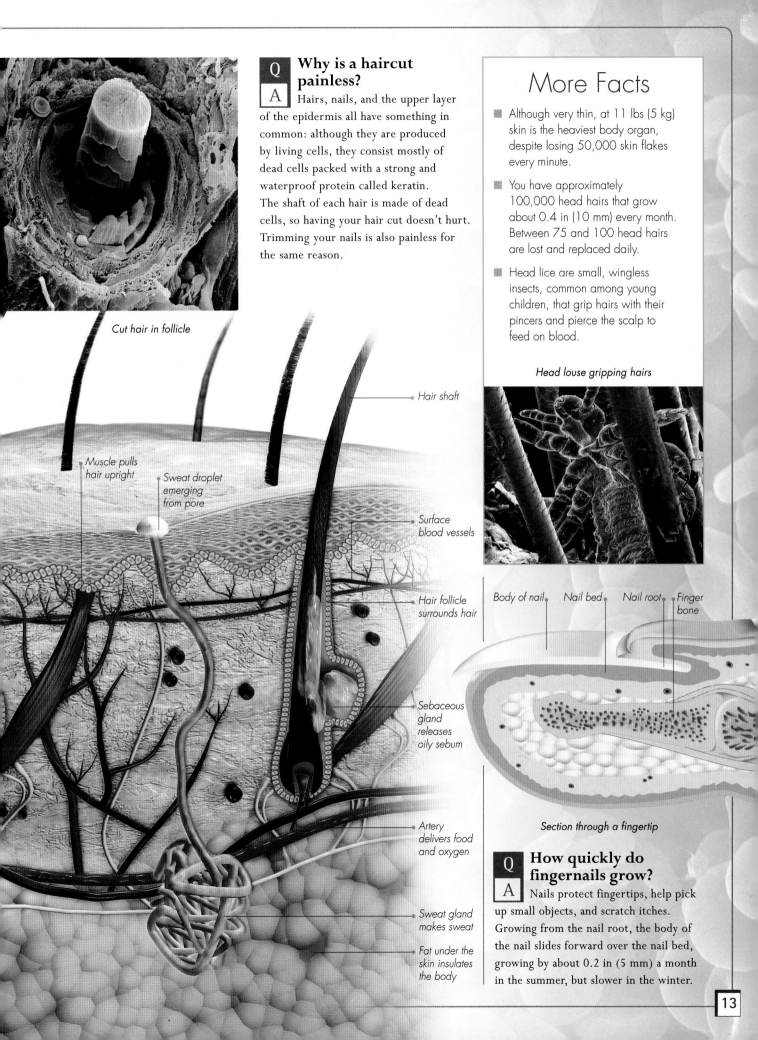

Q | Why is a haircut painless?

A Hairs, nails, and the upper layer of the epidermis all have something in common: although they are produced by living cells, they consist mostly of dead cells packed with a strong and waterproof protein called keratin. The shaft of each hair is made of dead cells, so having your hair cut doesn't hurt. Trimming your nails is also painless for the same reason.

Cut hair in follicle

Hair shaft

Muscle pulls hair upright

Sweat droplet emerging from pore

Surface blood vessels

Hair follicle surrounds hair

Sebaceous gland releases oily sebum

Artery delivers food and oxygen

Sweat gland makes sweat

Fat under the skin insulates the body

More Facts

- Although very thin, at 11 lbs (5 kg) skin is the heaviest body organ, despite losing 50,000 skin flakes every minute.

- You have approximately 100,000 head hairs that grow about 0.4 in (10 mm) every month. Between 75 and 100 head hairs are lost and replaced daily.

- Head lice are small, wingless insects, common among young children, that grip hairs with their pincers and pierce the scalp to feed on blood.

Head louse gripping hairs

Body of nail *Nail bed* *Nail root* *Finger bone*

Section through a fingertip

Q | How quickly do fingernails grow?

A Nails protect fingertips, help pick up small objects, and scratch itches. Growing from the nail root, the body of the nail slides forward over the nail bed, growing by about 0.2 in (5 mm) a month in the summer, but slower in the winter.

How many bones do I have?

Without its skeleton, your body would collapse in a floppy heap. This supportive framework is constructed from 206 bones and makes up about 20 percent of your body weight. Each bone is a living organ with a structure that makes it as strong as steel, but at a fraction of the weight. Your skeleton also surrounds and protects delicate organs, such as the brain and heart, and, when pulled by muscles, makes you move.

Human skeleton

Ribs protect the heart and lungs

Humerus, or upper arm bone

Frontal bone forms the forehead

Parietal bones at the top of the skull

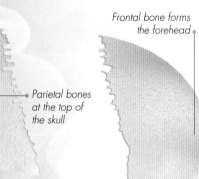

Temporal bones form the sides of the skull

Zygomatic, or cheek, bones

Phalanges, or finger bones

Femur, or thighbone, is the body's biggest and strongest bone

Occipital bone at the base of the skull

Exploded view of the skull

Backbone supports the upper body

Mandible, or lower jaw

Tibia, or shinbone

Metatarsals, or sole bones

Tarsals are the ankle and heel bones

Q A **Is the skull a single bone?**
A total of 22 bones form your skull. Eight of those bones, including the occipital and frontal bones, surround, support, and protect your brain. The other 14 bones, including the zygomatic bones, form the framework of your face. Most skull bones are locked together by immovable joints called sutures. Only the mandible moves, allowing you to eat, breathe, and speak.

Can bones bleed?

Bones are moist, living organs with their own network of blood vessels. So, yes, they can bleed. Each bone has an outer layer of hard, dense compact bone surrounding lighter spongy bone inside. This strong-but-light structure is built and maintained by bone cells, which are supplied by the blood vessels.

Blood vessels in compact bone

Spongy bone consists of struts and spaces

Bone marrow fills the central cavity

Bone structure

Compact bone is the hard, outer layer

Are male and female skeletons the same?

You can distinguish between male and female skeletons by looking at the pelvis. This basin-shaped structure attaches the thighbones to the body and supports organs in the abdomen. In women the opening in the center of the pelvis is wider than in men. This provides room for a baby's head to squeeze through during childbirth.

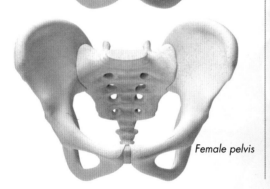

Male pelvis

Female pelvis

How do x-rays work?

By projecting this invisible type of radiation through the body and onto a photographic plate, doctors can see hard structures such as bones. Even though bones are very tough, fractures can happen if, for example, they suffer a sudden impact.

Artificially colored x-ray of fractured arm bones

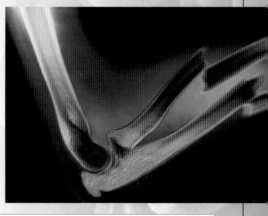

How do bones heal themselves?

If a bone is fractured, a self-repair system immediately springs into action. Blood leaking from damaged blood vessels clots in order to stop further bleeding. Then the rebuilding process, which takes weeks or months, begins. Doctors often line up the broken ends of the bones to make sure that the repair works correctly and is not the wrong shape.

1 Within hours of the fracture, a blood clot forms between bone ends, sealing off cut blood vessels.

2 After three weeks, fibrous tissue replaces the clot. New blood vessels supply bone-building cells.

3 After three months, new bone has replaced the fibrous tissue and the repair is almost complete.

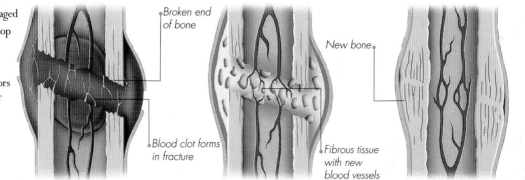

Broken end of bone

Blood clot forms in fracture

New bone

Fibrous tissue with new blood vessels

Why are muscles so important?

Eating your lunch or riding a bike would be impossible without muscles. They produce every movement that you make. Muscles are unique in their ability to contract, or get shorter, in order to create pulling power. There are three types of muscles. Skeletal muscles pull bones to move your body. Smooth muscles squeeze the walls of organs to, for example, push food along the small intestine. Cardiac muscle, found only in the heart, pumps blood.

Bundle of muscle fibers

Skeletal muscle

Muscle fiber

Myofibril

Blood vessel

Skeletal muscle structure

Q A What is inside a muscle?
Your skeletal muscles are made from long, cylindrical cells called muscle fibers. These are organized into bundles that run lengthwise down the muscle, and each fiber is packed with parallel, rodlike strands called myofibrils. These, in turn, contain overlapping filaments that interact to make muscles contract.

Q A How do muscles work?
Skeletal muscle contracts when your brain tells it to. Signals are carried from the brain by neurons or nerve cells (green), the ends of which form junctions with muscle fibers (red). The arrival of a nerve signal makes filaments inside the myofibrils slide over each other so that their muscle fibers, and therefore the muscle, get shorter and "pull" on a part of your body so that you move.

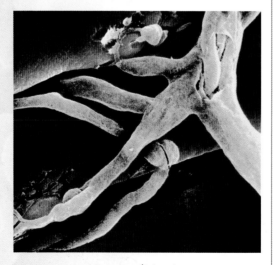

Nerve-muscle junction

Skeletal muscles (front view)

Deltoid raises the arm sideways, forward, and backward

Pectoralis major pulls the arm forward

Rectus abdominis bends the body forward

Quadriceps femoris straightens the knee

Gastrocnemius bends the foot downward

Tibialis anterior lifts the foot upward

How are muscles attached to bones?

At each end of a muscle, a cord or sheet called a tendon attaches it firmly to a bone. Each tendon is reinforced with parallel bundles of tough collagen fibers. This makes it incredibly strong so that, when a muscle contracts to pull a bone, its tendon does not tear. A tendon extends from a muscle, through the periosteum, and into the bone's outer layer, where it is firmly anchored.

Biceps femoris bends the arm at the elbow

Flexor carpi radialis bends the wrist

Muscle is covered by a protective sheath

Tendon is reinforced with tough collagen

Periosteum covers the outside of the bone

Connecting muscle to bone

What happens when I sleep?

As well as moving your body, muscles also maintain your posture. Muscles in your neck, back, and hips partially contract to keep your body upright and your head steady, whether you are standing or sitting. Called muscle tone, this partial contraction is constantly adjusted by your brain. When you fall asleep, muscle tone almost disappears. That's why, if you happen to fall asleep in a chair, your head flops to the side.

Falling asleep

Which muscles make me smile?

You have about 30 small muscles that produce a vast range of facial expressions and reveal to others how you are feeling. One end of your facial muscles are attached to the skin of your face, which they tug to create a particular look, be it grinning or frowning. Smiling muscles include the risorius, the two zygomaticus muscles, which pull the corner of your mouth upward and outward, and the levator labii superioris, which raises your upper lip.

Facial muscles

Frontalis raises the eyebrows

Zygomaticus minor

Zygomaticus major

Risorius pulls the mouth to the side

Orbicularis oris closes the eyes

Levator labii superioris

What makes athletes fast and flexible?

Anyone who exercises regularly and correctly can improve their fitness, which is a measure of how efficiently their body works. Athletes are very good examples of how this can be done. The joints between their bones, which allow the body to move, are very flexible. The muscles that pull on those bones in order to create movement are very strong. Athletes also have great stamina because their heart works efficiently to supply the muscles with energy.

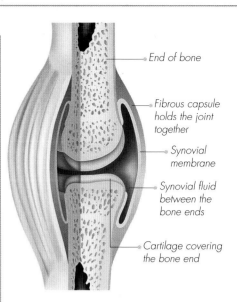

- End of bone
- Fibrous capsule holds the joint together
- Synovial membrane
- Synovial fluid between the bone ends
- Cartilage covering the bone end

Q How do joints move smoothly?

A Most of your body's 400 joints are free-moving synovial joints. They all share the basic structure that you can see above. The ends of the bone are coated with slippery cartilage and are separated by oily synovial fluid, released by the synovial membrane. The combination of cartilage and fluid allows the joint to move smoothly, without the bone ends rubbing together.

Athlete in action

Thigh muscle contracts to straighten the knee joint

Are there different types of joints?

There are six different types of synovial joints in your body. The shapes of their bones' ends and the way in which they fit together determine the range and freedom of movement allowed by each joint type. The ball and socket joint, for example, allows all-around movement.

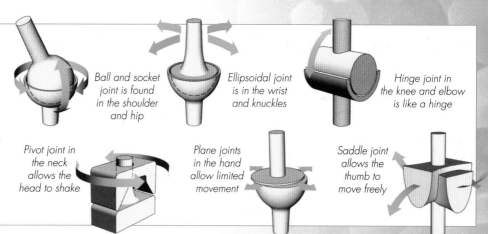

Ball and socket joint is found in the shoulder and hip

Ellipsoidal joint is in the wrist and knuckles

Hinge joint in the knee and elbow is like a hinge

Pivot joint in the neck allows the head to shake

Plane joints in the hand allow limited movement

Saddle joint allows the thumb to move freely

Q A How do muscles work with joints to move my body?

Muscles are attached to bones on either side of a joint. However, they can only pull, not push, so opposing sets of muscles are needed in order to produce movements in different directions. In the arm, for example, the biceps brachii contracts to bend the elbow joint, while the triceps brachii contracts to straighten it.

Triceps brachii contracts

Biceps brachii contracts

Opposing muscles

Q A Why do I get hot when I exercise?

To move your body, muscles convert chemical energy, in the form of fuels such as glucose, into movement energy. A byproduct of this conversion is heat. The more you exercise, the more heat your muscles release and the hotter you get. Thermography is a type of imaging that produces color-coded "heat pictures" called thermograms, which show how much heat is being released by the body.

X-ray of a dislocated finger joint

Q A What is a dislocated joint?

This x-ray shows two finger bones that have been forced out of line so that they no longer meet at a joint. In this situation the joint is said to be "dislocated". Dislocated joints are often caused by sporting injuries or falls. They are treated by a doctor who carefully moves the bones back into place.

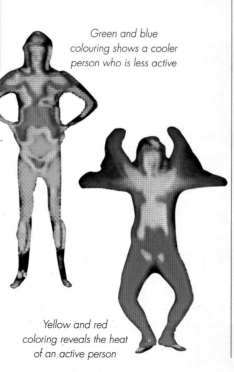

Green and blue colouring shows a cooler person who is less active

Yellow and red coloring reveals the heat of an active person

Q A Do joints wear out?

The cartilage that covers the ends of the bones in a joint can wear away with age. This makes the joint painful and much less flexible. One solution is to replace the worn-out joint with an artificial joint. Joints that can be replaced in this way include those in the knee, hip, shoulder, and finger.

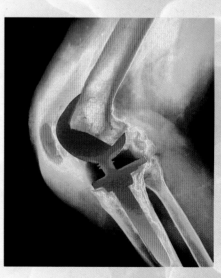

X-ray of an artificial knee joint

Fueling the Body

Why do I need to eat?

Every few hours we are driven by a feeling of hunger to eat food. Eating is essential because food contains the nutrients that the body needs in order to stay alive. Nutrients include carbohydrates and fats, which supply energy, proteins, which provide the raw materials for growth and repair, and vitamins and minerals, which cells need to work correctly. The body's digestive system digests, or breaks down, the complex molecules in food to release simple nutrients that the body can use. This process starts in the mouth.

This selection of vegetables is rich in vitamins and minerals

Basket of vegetables

Muscles are built from the raw materials and moved by the energy that food provides

Q A Why should I eat vegetables?

In order to stay healthy, you need to eat a balanced diet. That is, what you eat day by day should contain the right amounts of nutrients to provide energy, building materials, and other essentials. Vegetables are a key part of a balanced diet because they provide carbohydrates and certain vitamins and minerals.

Q A What does chewing do?

Before you can swallow food, you first have to chew it into small pieces. Your lips, cheeks, and tongue push food between your teeth. Powered by strong jaw muscles, front teeth slice food, while bulkier back teeth crush it into a paste. At the same time, your tongue mixes food with saliva.

How is food broken down?

Your teeth and stomach use muscle action to break down food into small particles. These particles are then targeted by chemical digesters called enzymes, especially in the small intestine. Enzymes speed up the breakdown of large food molecules into simple nutrients, such as glucose, that can be absorbed into the bloodstream.

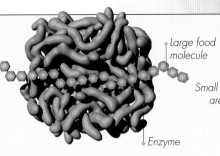

Large food molecule

Small molecules are released

Enzyme

Enzyme is unchanged

1 *An enzyme attaches to a complex food molecule and locks it in place.*

2 *The enzyme helps break down the complex molecule into simpler nutrients.*

More Facts

- In an average lifetime a person will eat about 25 tons of food, equivalent to the combined weight of five African bull elephants.

- We have two sets of teeth during our lifetime. The first set contains 20 milk, or baby, teeth. These are gradually replaced during childhood and teenage years by 32 adult teeth.

- We release two pints (one litre) of saliva daily. Saliva also cleans the mouth and contains a bacteria-killing chemical called lysozyme.

- Plaque is a mixture of food and bacteria that builds up and sticks to teeth that are not brushed regularly. Plaque bacteria feed on food remains, releasing acids that eat away at teeth and cause decay.

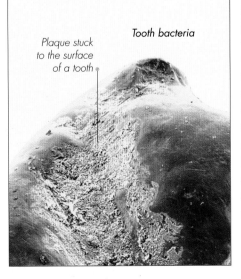

Plaque stuck to the surface of a tooth

Tooth bacteria

Salivary gland

Q A Why does my mouth water?

If you are hungry, the sight, smell, or thought of food triggers the release of saliva. This watery liquid is squirted into your mouth by three pairs of salivary glands (left, yellow). Saliva moistens food during chewing. It also contains an enzyme that digests starchy food and slimy mucus that binds chewed food particles together and makes them easier to swallow.

Q A What happens when I swallow?

Once food has been thoroughly chewed, your tongue pushes it backward. As soon as the slimy ball of food touches the back of your throat, it sets off an automatic reflex action. You briefly stop breathing, to stop food from going "down the wrong way," while food is pushed down your throat and into the esophagus. Muscles in the wall of your esophagus alternately contract (squeeze) and relax to move food downward to your stomach—a journey that takes just 10 seconds.

Food in the esophagus

Wall of esophagus

Muscles contract here

Muscles relax here

Food moves downward

What makes me burp?

Digestion really gets started in your stomach. There, chewed-up lumps of food are turned into a soupy mixture—a process that may produce gases that cause you to burp. Digestion is completed in the small intestine, where complex food substances are broken down into simple nutrients such as glucose. In the large intestine any leftover waste is turned into feces, ready to be pushed out of the body.

What is stomach acid?

Ten seconds after being swallowed, food arrives in the stomach, where it is mixed with gastric (stomach) juice. This highly acidic liquid is produced by millions of gastric glands deep in the stomach's lining. As well as a strong acid, gastric juice contains a protein-digesting enzyme called pepsin that only works in acidic conditions. Stomach acid also kills most harmful bacteria in food and drink.

Lining of stomach

Opening of gastric gland

What's the point of a pancreas?

Tucked under the stomach, your pancreas plays a key role in digestion. It releases pancreatic juice through a duct (tube) into the duodenum, the first section of the small intestine. This juice contains several enzymes that digest different types of food. The nearby gallbladder stores and releases bile, made by the liver, through the same duct, and this aids fat digestion.

Gallbladder

Pancreas releases several enzymes

How big is the small intestine?

The most important part of the digestive system, the small intestine is narrower but much longer than the large intestine. Its inner surface is folded and covered with tiny fingerlike villi. Enzymes on their surface complete the process of digestion, and villi provide a massive surface across which simple nutrients are absorbed into the bloodstream.

Villi lining the small intestine

Small intestine

How does the stomach work?

When food arrives in the stomach, its lower end—the exit into the small intestine—is closed off by a ring of muscle called the pyloric sphincter. The stomach's muscular walls mix food with gastric juice and churn it into a creamy paste. After three or four hours of mixing, partially digested food is released in small amounts into the small intestine.

1 As food arrives, the stomach expands. Its muscles squeeze food and mix it with gastric juice.

2 After hours of processing, creamy food is released in squirts into the small intestine.

Pyloric sphincter is open

Pyloric sphincter is closed

Stomach wall churns food

Muscles push out food

Stomach

Large intestine

Could I live without a liver?

Your liver is essential for life. Its busy cells perform more than 500 jobs that balance the chemical makeup of your blood. Those jobs include storing and processing recently digested nutrients—such as glucose, fats, vitamins, and minerals—arriving from the small intestine, removing poisons from the blood, and recycling worn-out red blood cells. These activities also release heat that helps keep your body's insides warm.

CT scan shows cross section through a liver

More Facts

- The pancreas releases two hormones, insulin and glucagon, into the bloodstream. These chemical messengers control levels of glucose—the body's main energy supply—in the blood.

- The liver is your body's largest internal organ. Only your skin is bigger and heavier.

- The small intestine is about 20 ft (6 m) long and 1 in (2.5 cm) wide. The large intestine is about 5 ft (1.5 m) long and 2 in (5 cm) wide.

- Billions of bacteria live harmlessly inside the colon, the longest part of the large intestine. They feed on undigested waste, give feces (poop) their color and smell, and make farts.

Bacteria inside the colon

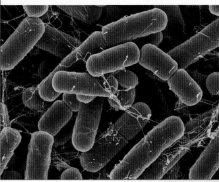

Video pill contains a tiny camera

Video pill

How long does digestion take?

The entire digestive process, from food being chewed to waste emerging from the other end, takes between one to two days. A device called a video pill takes a similar time, once swallowed, to travel from the mouth to the anus. It contains a tiny camera, a light source, and a transmitter that sends images of the inside of the intestines to a receiver outside a patient's body. Doctors then look at the images to see if the patient has any problems.

Why can't I breathe underwater?

Every time you breathe in, air is carried by your airways to your lungs. There, oxygen from the air enters your bloodstream to be carried to all your body cells. Cells need constant supplies of oxygen to release the energy that keeps them and you alive. That process also releases waste carbon dioxide, which you then breathe out. Your lungs only work in air —in order to breathe underwater, you would need gills like a fish.

Is it windy inside the windpipe?

As you breathe in and out, air rushes up and down your trachea, or windpipe, so it is very breezy in there. At its lower end, the trachea splits into two bronchi, one for each lung. Each bronchus then divides into smaller and smaller branches inside the lungs, getting air to every part.

What goes on inside the lungs?

The smallest branches of the bronchi, called bronchioles, end in bunches of tiny air sacs. There are 150 million of these microscopic air sacs, called alveoli, in each lung. Oxygen passes from the alveoli into the bloodstream to be carried to all the body's cells, while carbon dioxide moves in the opposite direction.

Alveolus surrounded by blood capillaries

Alveoli

Air space inside alveolus (cut open)

Right lung is slightly larger than the left

Trachea, or windpipe, carries air between the throat and lungs

Intercostal muscles connect and move the ribs

Ribs surround the lungs and aid breathing

Heart pumps blood to the lungs to pick up oxygen

Diaphragm is a dome-shaped muscle that helps breathing

Should I breathe through my nose?

It is preferable to inhale through your nose rather than through your mouth. Air passing through the nasal cavity—the space behind your nose—is automatically cleaned, moistened, and warmed. Sticky mucus and hairlike cilia lining the nasal cavity trap and dispose of dust and other particles that might otherwise damage your lungs.

Air turbulence caused by a sneeze

What causes hay fever?

We all inhale particles, such as pollen grains, when we breathe in. But some people react to these particles and develop an allergy called hay fever. This results in watery eyes, a runny, itchy nose, and sneezing. When somebody sneezes, a surge of air, released suddenly from the lungs, blasts through the nasal cavity to remove any irritations.

Cilia lining the nasal cavity

Lungs

Branching bronchi carry air to all parts of the left lung

Musician blows into a trumpet

How do musicians play and breathe at the same time?

Some musicians who play wind instruments, such as the trumpet or oboe, are able to use a technique called circular breathing. This allows them to play music without interruption for longer periods of time than they could with normal breathing. They learn to use their cheeks like bellows in order to maintain a flow of air through the instrument while at the same time inhaling air through their nose.

Why does my chest move when I breathe?

Your lungs cannot expand and shrink on their own. When you inhale, your diaphragm flattens and pushes downward while your ribs and chest move upward and outward. This makes your lungs expand so that air is sucked in. During exhalation, the diaphragm is pushed upward, the ribs move downward, your chest and lungs get smaller, and air is pushed out.

Inhalation (breathing in)

Exhalation (breathing out)

What is pee?

Your body's built-in waste disposal service, the urinary system, consists of two kidneys, two ureters, a bladder, and a urethra. The kidneys constantly process blood to keep its composition the same. They remove poisonous wastes produced by cells and surplus water from food and drink. Mixed together, the wastes and water form urine, which is released from your body when you pee.

Right kidney

Urinary system

Q **A** **How is urine made?**
Inside each kidney there are a million tiny, coiled tubes called nephrons. At one end of the nephron, fluid is filtered from the blood. As this fluid passes along the nephron, useful substances, such as glucose, pass back into the bloodstream. The remaining waste liquid, now called urine, flows out of the kidney and down the ureter to the bladder, where it is stored.

Nephrons filter blood to make urine

Ureter carries urine from the kidney to the bladder

Q **A** **What makes us feel the need to go to the bathroom?**
Your bladder has a stretchy wall that expands as it fills up with urine. You can see how much the bladder (green) expands in these x-rays (below). As the bladder fills up, stretch sensors in its wall send messages to your brain telling you that it's time to go to the bathroom.

Bladder is a stretchy, muscular storage "bag"

Sphincter muscle relaxes to release urine

Urethra carries urine to outside of the body

Full bladder

Empty bladder

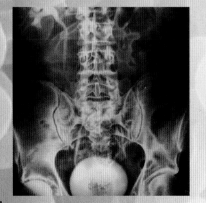

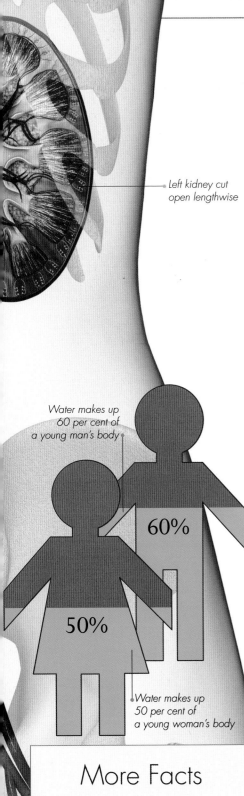

Left kidney cut
open lengthwise

A urine sample,
ready for testing

Water makes up
60 per cent of
a young man's body

60%

50%

Water makes up
50 per cent of
a young woman's body

Q **A** ## Why is urine yellow?

Urine contains various dissolved substances, one of which gives urine its yellow color. To help them discover why patients are sick, doctors check the levels of certain substances in urine to see if they are abnormal. A test stick is dipped into a patient's urine sample. Its colored bands detect specific substances and change colour to show how much of each is present.

Q **A** ## How much water is in my body?

Water is very important. It is a major part of blood, and without water, your cells would not work. A child's body is around 65 percent water. After puberty, water content depends on a person's sex. Women contain less water than men because they have more body fat—a tissue that contains little water.

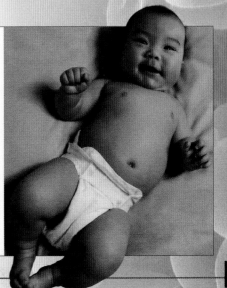

A sweating
rock climber

Q **A** ## What makes me feel thirsty?

Whenever you sweat, pee, or breathe out, your body loses some of its water. This makes your mouth feel dry and your blood more concentrated, which is detected by the "thirst center" in your brain. This thirst center is makes you feel thirsty, so that you feel the need to drink. The drink wets your mouth, quenches your thirst, and replaces the lost water.

More Facts

■ Babies can't control when they pee. Once a baby's bladder is full, it empties automatically.

■ Your kidneys process 3,080 pints (1,750 litres) of blood and filter about 317 pints (180 litres) of fluid into the nephrons, but release just 2.6 pints (1.5 litres) of urine per day.

■ Water makes up about 95 percent of urine. The major waste dissolved in urine is urea—a substance produced by liver cells.

■ To keep your water content the same, the kidneys release more, diluted urine if you have drunk lots of fluid and less urine that is more concentrated if you are dehydrated and sweating.

BRAINPOWER

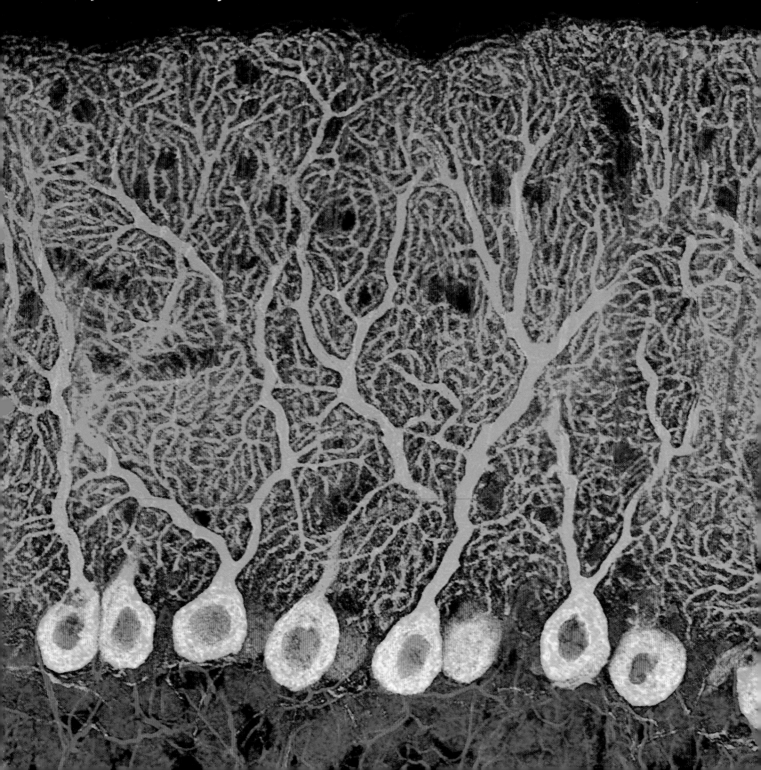

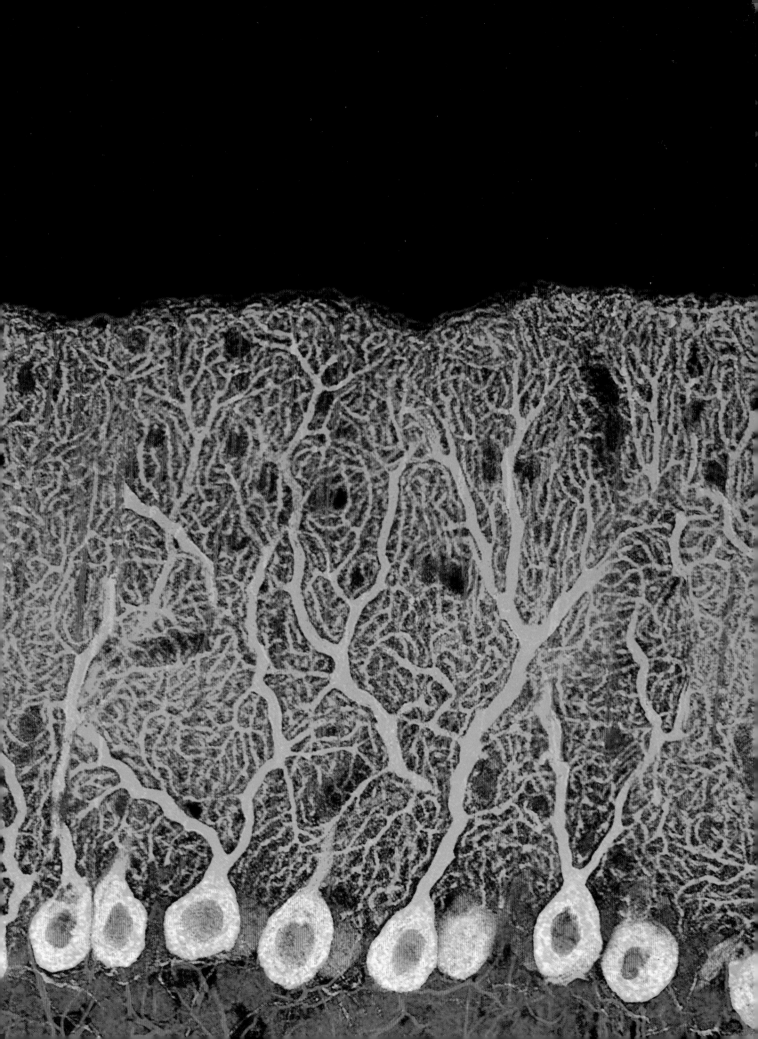

Do smart people have bigger brains?

The nervous system controls and coordinates your body's activities with split-second timing. It collects information about what is happening inside and outside your body and sends it along nerves and the spinal cord to your brain. There, the information is processed, enabling you to think, feel, remember, and move. Your brain's size doesn't affect any of this—having a bigger brain does not make you any smarter.

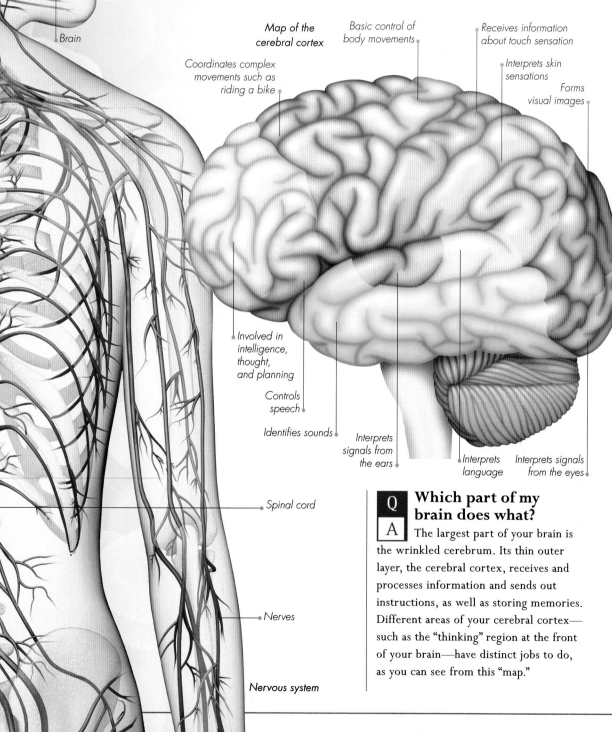

Brain

Map of the cerebral cortex

Coordinates complex movements such as riding a bike

Basic control of body movements

Receives information about touch sensation

Interprets skin sensations

Forms visual images

Involved in intelligence, thought, and planning

Controls speech

Identifies sounds

Interprets signals from the ears

Interprets language

Interprets signals from the eyes

Spinal cord

Nerves

Nervous system

Q / A Which part of my brain does what?

The largest part of your brain is the wrinkled cerebrum. Its thin outer layer, the cerebral cortex, receives and processes information and sends out instructions, as well as storing memories. Different areas of your cerebral cortex—such as the "thinking" region at the front of your brain—have distinct jobs to do, as you can see from this "map."

How do I react so quickly?

Q
A Your nervous system is constructed from a massive network of interconnected cells called neurons. The brain alone contains 100 billion neurons. Each neuron has a long, narrow extension called a nerve fiber that generates and transmits electrical signals, called impulses, at very high speeds. This allows you to instantly react to events, even when the signal has to travel all the way from your big toe to your brain.

Neurons in the brain

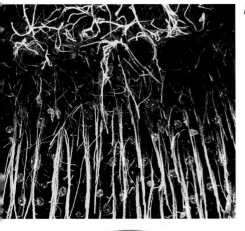

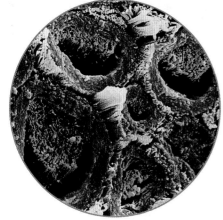

Cross section through nerve

What is a nerve?

Q
A Nerves are the cables of the nervous system. Their "wires" are the long nerve fibers (green) that carry high-speed signals. Bundles of nerve fibers are protected by tough but bendable sheaths (purple). Nerves relay information from sensors to the spinal cord and brain about what is happening to the body. They also carry instructions the opposite way to muscles and other organs.

Painting with the left hand

How can reflexes protect me from danger?

Q
A If you touch something sharp or very hot, you automatically pull your hand away without thinking about it. This is an example of a reflex—an action that is rapid, unchanging, and protects us from harm. Pain signals from your fingers travel to your spinal cord. This sends instructions to your arm muscles to move your hand at the same time that signals reach your brain so that you feel pain.

Withdrawal reflex

Why are some people left-handed?

Q
A The main part of your brain, the cerebrum, has left and right sides. The left side controls the right side of your body and vice versa. Normally, the left side dominates, which explains why most people are right-handed. But in about 10 percent of people, the right side is dominant, so they are left-handed.

More Facts

- Your brain makes up just 2 percent of your body weight but uses 20 percent of your oxygen intake to release energy to keep it working.

- Busy brain neurons create patterns of electrical activity called brain waves, which can be detected by attaching electrodes to the scalp.

Detecting brain waves

- Your brain doesn't turn off when you sleep, although its brain waves change. At night your brain sorts and stores information, making you dream.

- The left side of your cerebrum deals with math, language, and problem solving. The right side focuses on art, music, and creativity.

Why can't I see in the dark?

Vision is our most important sense. It allows us to see our surroundings. The sense organs responsible for vision are the eyes. Moving constantly, the eyes collect light and focus it onto receptor cells. These cells send signals to the brain, which creates images that we can see. In the dark there is little or no light, so we are unable to see.

Retina contains light receptors

Optic nerve carries nerve signals to the brain

Fovea is the most sensitive part of the retina

Structure of the eye

Q A Why do my pupils change size?

Your colored irises automatically control the size of your pupils and, therefore, the amount of light that enters your eyes. Without this control, you would be dazzled in bright light and unable to see in dim light. Circular muscle fibers in your irises close your pupils in bright light, and spokelike radial muscle fibers contract to open your pupils in dim light.

Radial muscle fibers relax

Circular muscle fibers contract

Radial muscle fibers contract

Circular muscle fibers relax

Sclera is the tough outer layer

Muscle moves the eyeball

Light receptor cells

Cone

Rod

Q A How do we see in color?

The retina contains two types of light receptor cells. About 120 million rods work best in dim light and enable you to see in shades of gray. Seven million cones, mostly found in the fovea directly behind the lens, allow you to see the color and detail of what you are looking at.

Q A Is an eye similar to a camera?

Cameras use lenses to focus light rays from an object to form an image on a light-sensitive surface. The eyes are no different. Light rays from an object are focused automatically, whatever its distance from the eyes, by the cornea and lens to form an upside-down image on the retina. This sends signals to the brain, which enables you to "see" the object the right way around.

Lens

Cornea

Retina

Object

Light rays

Upside-down image

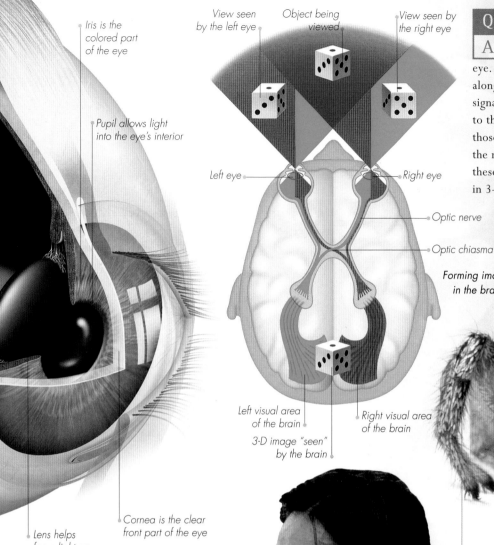

Iris is the colored part of the eye

View seen by the left eye

Object being viewed

View seen by the right eye

Pupil allows light into the eye's interior

Left eye

Right eye

Optic nerve

Optic chiasma

Forming images in the brain

Left visual area of the brain

Right visual area of the brain

3-D image "seen" by the brain

Lens helps focus light on the retina

Cornea is the clear front part of the eye

How can I see in 3-D?

Looking at this dice, your left eye has a different view from your right eye. Information about each view passes along the optic nerves. At the optic chiasma signals from the left side of each eye go to the left visual area of your brain, while those from the right side of each eye go to the right visual area. Your brain compares these signals to recreate the original object in 3-D and to figure out how faraway it is.

Jumping spider

What makes us cry?

Tear glands below your eyebrows produce watery tears that wash over your eyeballs. There are three types of tears. Basal tears are released constantly to wash away dust, moisten your eyes, and kill bacteria. Reflex tears are a response to irritants such as onion odors or bright light. Emotional tears, unique to humans, flow when you are very sad, happy, or in pain and contain natural painkillers.

Emotional crying

More Facts

■ Jumping spiders have eight eyes, including two large, forward-facing eyes that enable it to judge distances very accurately and pounce on unwary prey.

■ Your eyes contain more than 70 percent of your body's sensory receptors. They can detect and distinguish between about 10,000 different colors.

■ Just one sixth of the eyeball is visible from the outside. The rest is protected inside the bony eye socket, with extra protection from the eyelids, eyelashes, and eyebrows.

■ Your eyes are never still. As well as following moving objects, they also make tiny jumping movements called saccades that scan objects in view.

How did I hear what you said?

Your ears pick up a vast array of sounds, including speech. The only visible parts of your ears are the flaps, called pinnae, on the sides of your head. The rest of the ear lies protected inside the bones of the skull. There, sounds are converted into nerve signals that your brain turns back into recognizable sounds that you "hear," and fluid-filled canals help you keep your balance.

Pinna

Three semicircular canals

Ossicles

Outer ear canal

Structure of the ear

Eardrum

Oval window

Eardrum with malleus (ossicle)

Q Can insects crawl into my ear?

A The ear canal carries sound waves toward the eardrum. The skin that lines its outer section has tiny hairs and produces earwax, which cleans and moistens the ear canal. Deterred by the hairs and earwax, insects rarely crawl inside the ear canal—but if they do, they cannot get any farther than the eardrum.

What are sound waves?

Anything that moves or vibrates creates waves of pressure, called sound waves, that travel through the air. On entering your ear, they make the eardrum vibrate. This, in turn, sets up pressure waves in the fluid-filled cochlea of the inner ear. These bend the tiny "hairs" on the cochlea's hair cells, causing them to send signals to the hearing part of your brain.

Hair cells in the cochlea

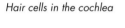

Cochlear nerve carries signals to the brain

Cochlea

Eustachian tube

Are there any bones in my ear?

Linking the eardrum to the inner ear are three small bones, or ossicles, individually named the malleus (hammer), incus (anvil), and stapes (stirrup) after their shapes. The smallest, the stapes is even tinier than the incus shown here. The ossicles form a bony chain that transmits sound vibrations from the eardrum to the oval window—the entrance to the inner ear.

Incus bone on a fingertip

Listening to an mp3 player

Can loud noise damage my ears?

Your ears can distinguish between a massive range of sound volumes and have a built-in mechanism to protect the inner ear from sudden loud noises. But long-term exposure to loud sounds, such as constantly listening to loud music through earphones, can damage the cochlea's delicate hair cells and lead to deafness.

How do ears help us balance?

The inner ear contains three semicircular canals, arranged at right angles to each other. These, and other inner ear sensors, keep your brain updated about the movement and position of your head. Your brain uses this information, together with input from your eyes, to tell your muscles what to do, in order to keep you balanced.

Balancing gymnast

More Facts

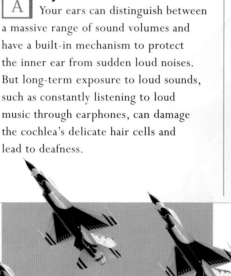

- The Eustachian tube connects your ear to your throat and keeps air pressure inside and outside the ear equal. A sudden pressure change, such as when a plane takes off, makes hearing difficult. But if you yawn or swallow, the tube widens to equalize pressure, causing your ears to pop.

Planes taking off

- Sounds reach one ear a split second before the other. This allows your brain to figure out which direction the sounds came from.

- Younger people can hear a much wider range of sounds than older people can.

- Animals such as cats and bats can hear very high-pitched sounds that we cannot.

Why does candy taste sweet?

Being able to smell and taste allows us to enjoy food and drink and many other aspects of life. The senses of smell and taste are closely linked; both are located in the head—one in the nose and the other in the mouth. Both detect chemicals that are carried in the air (smell) or in food (taste). They also help us distinguish between the sweetness of candy, and the bitterness of foods that might be poisonous.

Smell receptors at the end of olfactory (smell) nerve branches in the nasal cavity

Bitter tastes are detected here

Tongue

Nerve from the taste buds at the rear of the tongue

Nerve carries touch signals

Nerve from the taste buds at the front of the tongue

All five basic tastes are detected by taste buds all over the tongue

Fungiform papilla

Filiform papilla

Nasal cavity carries air

Surface of the tongue

Q&A How do taste buds work?

Your tongue has about 10,000 tiny receptors called taste buds that detect taste molecules in food. Taste buds detect five basic tastes—sweet, sour, salty, bitter, and umami—a savory, meaty taste. Two nerves carry signals from the taste buds to the brain. Some parts of the tongue may be more sensitive to certain tastes. Other receptors in the tongue detect the texture and temperature of food.

Q&A What are the tiny bumps on my tongue?

Look closely at your tongue in a mirror and you will see that it is covered with tiny bumps, called papillae. Fungiform ("mushroom-shaped") papillae house the taste buds in their sides and tops, as do the large vallate papillae right at the back of the tongue. The more slender filiform papillae do not have taste buds. They contain touch receptors and help your tongue grip food as you chew it.

Nerve that carries signals from the front two thirds of the tongue

Nerve that carries signals from the rear one third of the tongue

Surface of the tongue

How do I smell things?

Q **A** Smelling happens in the lining of the roof of your nasal cavity— the space behind your nose. Sticking out from the lining are the tips of smell receptors, which look like this (see below). Each tip has several hairlike cilia. Breathed-in molecules dissolve in watery mucus and stick to these cilia. This causes the smell receptors to send signals to the brain, which identifies what you are smelling.

Can we smell danger?

Q **A** As well as helping you enjoy delicious food or pick up the scent of flowers, your sense of smell has another important role to play. The smell of smoke, for example, warns you that something may be on fire and that you need to take action. Food that looks fine but smells terrible should put you off eating it in case it is poisonous.

Smell receptor

Is smell more important than taste?

Q **A** Of the two senses, smell is the dominant partner because you can distinguish many more odors than tastes. When you eat food such as popcorn, the combination of smell and taste allows you to sense and appreciate its flavors. But if, for example, you have a bad cold and lose your sense of smell, food tastes very bland, and if you close your eyes, is difficult to identify.

Brain stem

Smell and taste detection

Fresh popcorn

More Facts

- People who work as perfumers have a "super sense" of smell that enable them to identify and distinguish between subtle fragrances.

- Other people with smell and taste "super senses" are employed as tea, wine, or food tasters. They are born with this exceptional ability.

- Your millions of smell receptors can detect more than 10,000 different smells, but your taste buds can only detect five different tastes.

- Some scents can be detected at very low concentrations, including methyl mercaptan—the chemical added to odorless natural gas to make it smell.

PUMPING BLOOD

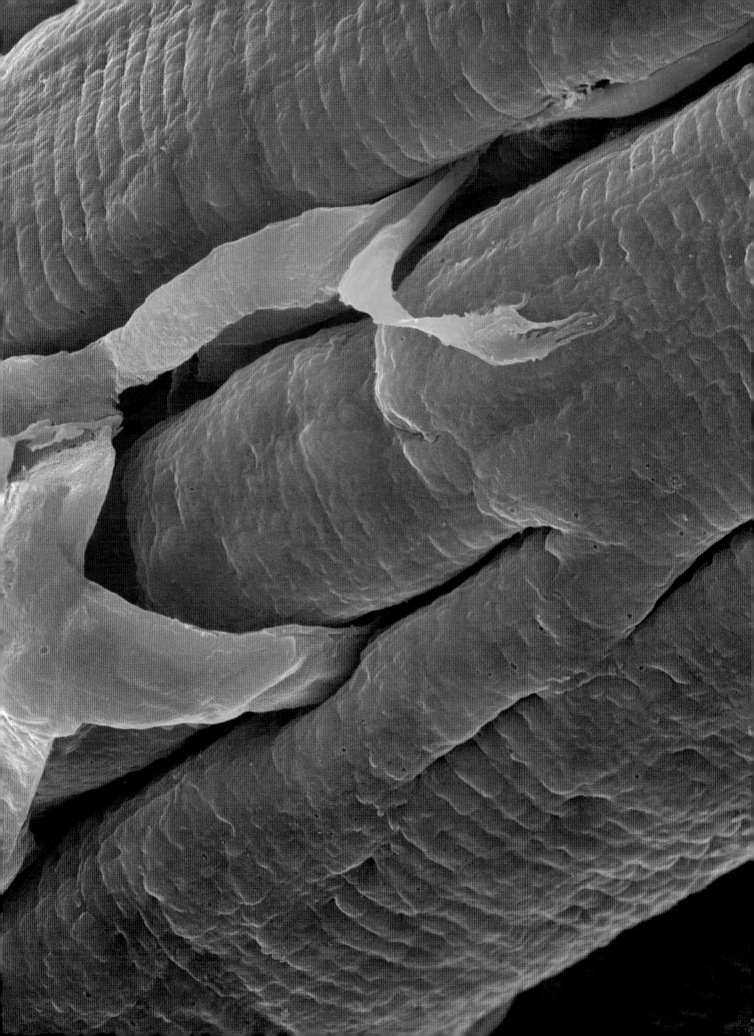

Blood cells

Neutrophils
hunt and eat
invading germs

Red blood cells carry
oxygen from the lungs
to the tissues

...destroy pathogens

Lymphocytes are
white blood cells
that release
germ-killing chemicals

Why is blood red?

Your body's cells need a constant supply of food, oxygen, and other essentials, as well as a prompt removal of wastes, in order to stay alive. Blood provides this delivery and disposal service as it flows around the body. Billions of oxygen-carrying red blood cells give blood its red color. Blood also contains white blood cells that defend your body against invading pathogens or germs.

Plasma—55%

White blood cells
and platelets—1%

Red blood
cells—44%

Q | A What is blood made up of?

If a tube full of blood is spun at high speed in a centrifuge, its different parts separate. Blood cells and platelets sink to the bottom. At the top is yellowish plasma, the liquid in which blood cells normally float. Plasma consists of water and more than 100 dissolved substances, including nutrients, wastes, and hormones.

Q | A Where are blood cells made?

Bones contain a jellylike material called bone marrow. Adults have two types: yellow bone marrow, found in long bones, stores fat; red bone marrow, found mostly in flat bones, produces all types of blood cells, including platelets. The bones that contain red marrow are colored pink on this skeleton. In babies, all bone marrow is red.

Red bone marrow

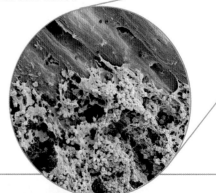

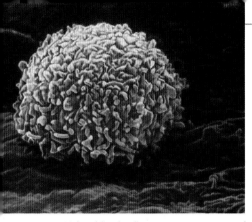

White blood cell

Are white blood cells really white?

This neutrophil has been colored to make it stand out, but in real life it is transparent, like other types of white blood cells. They are called "white" because they are not red, and also because they form a thin, white layer when blood is spun in a centrifuge tube. Like other white blood cells, neutrophils protect the body against infections.

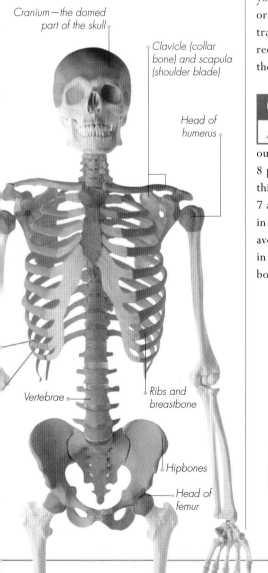

Cranium—the domed part of the skull

Clavicle (collar bone) and scapula (shoulder blade)

Head of humerus

Vertebrae

Ribs and breastbone

Hipbones

Head of femur

Transfusion bags containing blood

Why are there different blood groups?

Your red blood cells carry one, both, or neither of two tiny markers called A and B. Whether you do or don't have these markers determines whether you belong to blood group A, B, AB, or O. To avoid problems during blood transfusions (transfers), a person should receive blood from someone of the same blood group.

How much blood do I have?

If all the blood was drained out of your body, you would be about 8 percent lighter in weight. In adults this percentage amounts to between 7 and 8.8 pints (4 and 5 litres) of blood in women and, because they are bigger on average, 8.8 to 10.5 pints (5 to 6 litres) in men. The volume of blood in your body is controlled by your kidneys.

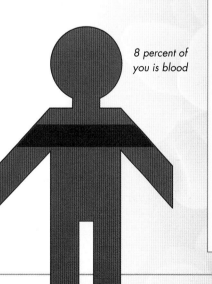

8 percent of you is blood

More Facts

- A single tiny drop of blood contains 250 million red blood cells, 375,000 white blood cells, and 16 million platelets.

- Red blood cells have no nucleus and a life span of 120 days. Two million new red blood cells are made by bone marrow every second.

Rosy periwinkle

- Leukemia is a disease, sometimes fatal, in which too many abnormal white blood cells are produced. Drugs extracted from the rosy periwinkle, a rainforest plant, have been used to successfully treat leukemia.

- Red blood cells contain hemoglobin, a red-colored protein that carries oxygen. A single red blood cell contains 250 million hemoglobin molecules.

How fast does my heart beat?

At the core of your body's blood transportation system is a muscular pump—the heart. The heart has two sides, left and right, each with an upper and lower chamber , the atrium and ventricle. The heart beats about 70 times per minute to pump blood to your cells, speeding up when necessary to meet increased demand. During an average lifetime, the heart beats more than 2.5 billion times without taking a rest.

Superior vena cava brings oxygen-poor blood from the upper body

Valve guards the exit from the right ventricle

Right atrium receives oxygen-poor blood

Q A Does the heart have its own blood supply?

The muscular wall of your heart needs an uninterrupted supply of fuel and oxygen to keep it beating. But it can't get these supplies from the blood that gushes through its chambers. Instead, it has its own special supply: two coronary arteries, shown here in this cast, branch repeatedly to carry oxygen-rich blood throughout the heart's wall.

Cardiac (heart) muscle

Cast of coronary arteries

Left coronary artery

Q A What's special about heart muscle?

In a lifetime of beating your heart never takes a break. Cardiac muscle never tires, contracting regularly and automatically to pump blood. A tiny section of the wall of the right atrium acts as a "pacemaker." It sends out signals that make the network of cardiac muscle cells contract at the same rate.

Valve between the atrium and ventricle

Right ventricle pumps blood to the lungs

Inferior vena cava carries oxygen-poor blood from the abdomen and legs

Right coronary artery

What happens during a heartbeat?

If you listen to, or feel, your heart beating, every heartbeat probably feels like a single event. In fact, each one is made up of three separate, precisely timed stages. Electrical signals spread through the heart's muscular wall, ensuring that first the atria and then the ventricles contract to pump blood through and out of the heart. Valves ensure that blood flow is always in the same direction.

1 Your heart's muscular wall is relaxed, and blood from the lungs and the body flows, respectively, into the left and right atria.

2 Left and right atria contract together, forcing blood through the valves that separate them from their ventricles. Other valves remain closed.

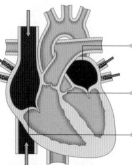

Left atrium fills with oxygen-rich blood

Valves close to stop backflow into the ventricles

Right atrium fills with oxygen-poor blood

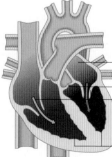

Right atrium contracts at the same time as the left

Valves remain closed

Valves between the atria and ventricles open

Ventricles fill with blood

Aorta carries oxygen-rich blood from the heart

Pulmonary artery takes oxygen-poor blood to the lungs

Left atrium receives oxygen-rich blood

Pulmonary veins carry oxygen-rich blood from the lungs

Left ventricle has a thicker wall than the right because it pumps blood farther

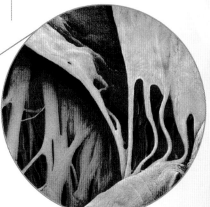

How the heart works

Heartstrings

Do heartstrings really exist?

Q / **A** If someone "tugs at your heartstrings," it means that you feel sympathy for them. It's just an expression, but there are also real heartstrings. When your ventricles contract, these cords tug at the valves between the atria and ventricles. This stops the valves from turning inside out like umbrellas in a gale.

Why does my heart beat faster when I run?

Q / **A** Your muscles need energy to move you. This energy is generated using glucose and oxygen, which are delivered by the blood. The more active you are and the more strenuous the exercise, the harder your muscles work and the more energy they need. To supply this demand, your heart beats faster in order to pump more blood to your muscles to meet their need for extra glucose and oxygen.

Strenuous exercise

What do doctors hear through a stethoscope?

Q / **A** Every time your heart beats, it produces sounds. A short "dup" sound is created when the valves guarding the heart's exits close as the ventricles relax. A longer "lub" sound is made when the ventricles contract and valves between atria and ventricles slam shut. By listening to heart sounds, doctors can check whether valves are doing their job correctly.

Scan of relaxed heart

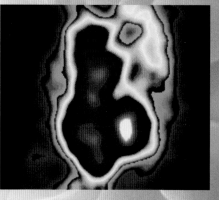

Scan of contracted heart

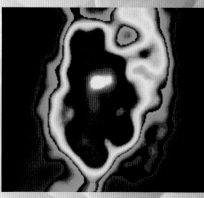

3 The two ventricles contract together, pushing blood to the lungs and body. Valves between atria and ventricles close to prevent backflow.

Blood pumped to the body

Blood pumped to the lungs

Valves guarding the exits from the ventricles open

Valves between the atria and ventricles shut

Ventricles contract together

What journey does my blood take?

Pumped by the heart, blood circulates in one direction around the body to deliver supplies to all body cells. This circulatory system has two "loops." One carries oxygen-poor blood (blue) from the heart to the lungs to pick up oxygen. The other sends out oxygen-rich blood (red) to the tissues through the aorta and returns oxygen-poor blood to the heart through the large vena cava veins.

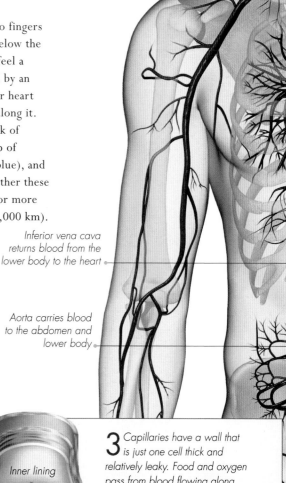

Circulatory system

Common carotid artery carries blood to the head and brain

Subclavian artery carries blood to the arm

Inferior vena cava returns blood from the lower body to the heart

Aorta carries blood to the abdomen and lower body

What is a pulse?

Q A If you hold the tips of two fingers against your wrist, just below the base of your thumb, you should feel a regular "pulse." This is produced by an artery expanding every time your heart beats and forcing blood along it. You have a vast network of blood vessels, made up of arteries (red), veins (blue), and tiny capillaries. Altogether these blood vessels stretch for more than 60,000 miles (100,000 km).

Blood vessels serving the upper body and head

Superior vena cava

Right side of the heart pumps oxygen-poor blood to the lungs

Blood vessels in the liver

Inferior vena cava

Blood vessels in the lower body and legs

Blood vessels in the lung

Left side of the heart pumps oxygen-rich blood to the body

Aorta is the biggest artery

Blood vessels in the stomach and intestines

Blood flow around the body

What is the difference between arteries and veins?

There are three types of blood vessels in your body—arteries, veins, and capillaries—each one with their own distinct structure. Arteries and veins are linked by a network of capillaries that pass through all body tissues.

1 Arteries carry oxygen-rich blood from the heart to the tissues. They have a thick wall that is both muscular and stretchy to withstand the high blood pressure created when the heart beats.

2 Veins have thin walls and carry oxygen-poor blood under low pressure from the tissues toward the heart. Valves inside veins prevent blood from flowing backward.

3 Capillaries have a wall that is just one cell thick and relatively leaky. Food and oxygen pass from blood flowing along the capillaries to the surrounding tissue cells.

Inner lining

Muscle layer

Outer protective layer

Muscle layer

Stretchy layer

Inner lining

Valve flap stops blood flowing the wrong way

Outer layer

Capillary wall allows some substances to pass through easily

Nucleus of a cell in a capillary wall

46

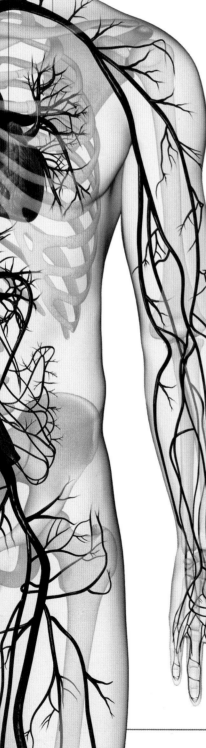

Heart pumps blood

Subclavian vein carries blood from the arm and shoulder

Cut-open capillary

Q A How wide are capillaries?

Ten capillaries placed side by side would be as thick as a hair from your head. Or, put another way, these tiniest of blood vessels are just wider than a red blood cell. Since red blood cells have to travel in single file along capillaries, it gives them more time to release oxygen into the surrounding tissues.

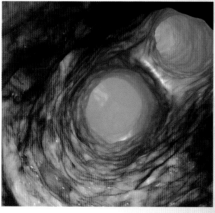

Inside an artery

Q A How fast does my blood flow?

When blood emerges from the heart, it races along the largest arteries at around 3 ft (1 m) per second. It slows down in smaller arteries and becomes even more sluggish as it travels along capillaries and veins. That said, a red blood cell takes, on average, less than one minute to get around the circulatory circuit. The slick lining of blood vessels ensures that blood flows smoothly.

Q A Why do people get frostbite?

When it's cold, the blood vessels supplying your skin temporarily get narrower so that less blood flows through them. This reduces heat loss through the skin, especially from exposed parts such as the fingers. But if the body is exposed to freezing conditions for long periods, narrowed blood vessels starve skin cells of vital supplies, resulting in painful frostbite.

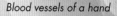

Blood vessels of a hand

Q A What is blood pressure?

It may have a long name but this machine (below) has a straightforward role, measuring your blood pressure. This is the pressure, or "push", on an artery's wall, produced when your heart beats. Blood pressure provides the driving force that keeps blood moving around your body. But if it is too high for long periods, it can cause health problems.

Sphygmomanometer

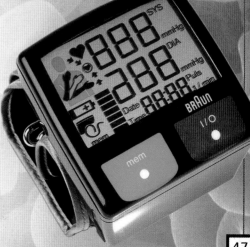

How does my body protect itself?

You are constantly exposed to germs that will make you sick if they get inside your body. Various defense mechanisms stop this from happening. Your skin, for example, is a germ-proof barrier. If germs do get in, they are destroyed by macrophages and lymphocytes—white blood cells found in your blood—and in your body's drainage network, the lymphatic system (below).

Q **What are germs?**

A Also called pathogens, germs are microorganisms— living things that can only be seen using a microscope—that cause disease. That is, they stop your body from working normally. Germs include the viruses that give you the flu or a cold and the bacteria that cause stomachaches. Left to their own devices, they would multiply inside your body and cause great harm.

Flu virus particle

Tonsils trap breathed-in germs

Lymph drains into this vein

Thymus gland "trains" defense cells

Thoracic duct collects lymph from the legs and abdomen

Lymph vessel carries lymph toward the main ducts

Lymph node "filters" lymph and contains macrophages and lymphocytes

Lymph capillary collects lymph from the tissues

E.coli bacteria

How do white blood cells kill bacteria?

Macrophages like this one are white blood cells that specialize in destroying bacteria by eating them. This ruthless hunter tracks down invaders by following the chemical trails that they leave behind. The macrophage then sends out projections that stick to and surround a bacterium and pulls the germ inside it. Once inside the macrophage, the bacterium us doused in powerful enzymes that digest and kill it.

Macrophage (gold) attacking bacteria (blue)

More Facts

▪ Protists are single-celled organisms, and some of them are germs. Plasmodium, for example, is a protist that causes malaria. Biting mosquitoes spread it from person to person, and it multiplies inside their red blood cells.

▪ Once you have had a particular disease, your immune system responds much faster to another attack of the same pathogens, so you rarely get the same disease twice.

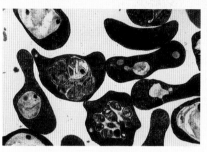
Plasmodium protists inside red blood cells

▪ Your tears, saliva, and sweat contain germ-killing chemicals, while stomach acid destroys bacteria or viruses that you swallow in food or drink.

Why does a doctor take your temperature?

Under normal conditions, your body's internal temperature is about 98.6°F (37°C). But if you are infected by bacteria or viruses, your body gets hotter, producing a fever. This helps fight infection because germs cannot multiply and spread at higher temperatures.

Taking a temperature

Does my body remember different germs?

Your body has an army of powerful defenders. Lymphocytes are a type of white blood cell that "remember" a germ's identity and release disease-fighting chemicals called antibodies to target specific germs. Antibodies do not destroy germs; they bind to their prey and mark them for destruction by macrophages.

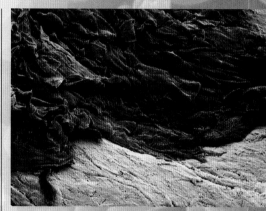
Close-up view of a scab (red)

How does a scab form?

A built-in repair mechanism acts swiftly to plug leaks from damaged blood vessels. If, for example, you cut yourself and start bleeding, a jellylike clot forms at the wound site to seal the holes in blood vessels. The clot dries out to form a protective scab that stays in place on the skin until the tissues underneath it have been repaired.

Antibodies (blue and pink) surround a bacterium

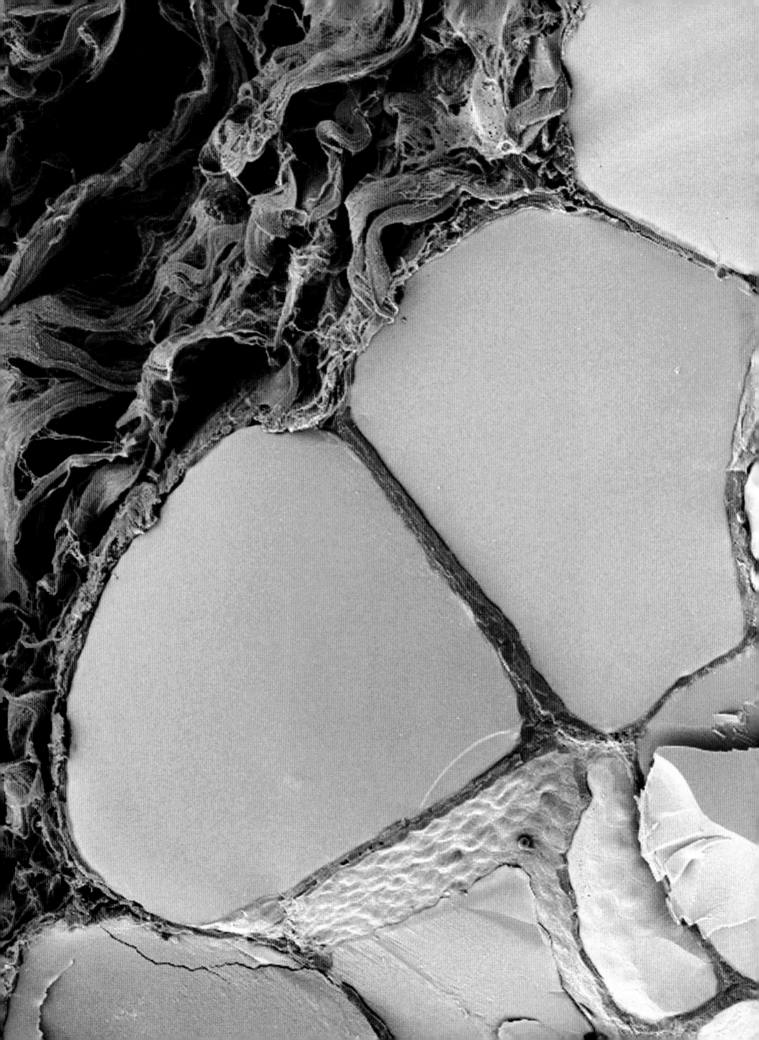

LIFE STORY

Sperm is streamlined with a beating tail

Egg is much bigger than sperm and surrounded by a protective layer

Sperm penetrating an egg

What is fertilization?

The job of the reproductive system is to produce babies. Unlike other body systems, male and female reproductive systems are very different. But, in adults, both produce special sex cells—eggs in women and sperm in men—that contain the genetic material to make a person. If sperm and egg meet and fuse, fertilization occurs. Genetic instructions from both parents combine to produce a new individual. The female reproductive system also provides a safe place for the baby to develop during the nine months of pregnancy.

Q A Where does fertilization occur?
The female reproductive system consists of two ovaries, two fallopian tubes, the uterus, and the vagina—a tube that connects the uterus to outside of the body. Each month one of the ovaries releases a mature egg into the fallopian tube. If the egg meets sperm within one day of its release, fertilization will happen. Once a sperm has penetrated the outer covering of the egg, its nucleus fuses with the egg's nucleus to form a fertilized egg.

Female reproductive system

Fallopian tube carries egg from the ovary to the uterus

Ovaries produce and store eggs, then release them

Male reproductive system

Ductus deferens carries sperm from testes

Seminal vesicles and prostate gland release fluids that feed and activate sperm

Urethra carries sperm to outside of the body

Testes hang outside the body in a skin pouch

Penis transfers sperm to the vagina

Q A Where are sperm made?
Males have two plum-sized testes that contain masses of tiny, coiled tubules. These are the sperm "factories" inside which cells divide to produce immature sperm. It takes 20 days for sperm to mature before they are pushed into the ductus deferens—the tube that delivers them to the penis. Together, the testes, penis, and the tubes that link them make up the male reproductive system.

What happens next?

The fertilized egg moves along the fallopian tube toward the uterus. About 36 hours after fertilization, it divides into two identical cells. From then on, division happens every 12 hours, doubling the number of cells present to four, eight, and so on. Four days after fertilization, a ball of 32 cells is ready to leave the fallopian tube. Two days later, inside the uterus a hollow ball of cells called a blastocyst has been formed.

2-cell stage

32-cell stage

Uterus lining has a lot of blood vessels

Embryo develops from these cells

Yolk sac feeds the embryo in its first weeks

Amnion forms protective bag around the embryo

Ten days after fertilization

Where does a baby grow?

Just over one week after fertilization, the blastocyst burrows into the soft lining of the uterus to continue its development. The blastocyst's inner cell mass forms the embryo; the rest of it nurtures and protects the growing embryo, partially forming the placenta and umbilical cord that will obtain food and oxygen from the mother's blood supply. By eight weeks after fertilization the fetus, as it is now called, is recognizably human and consists of billions of cells.

Uterus has a thick, muscular wall

Uterus lining is where embryo develops

Vagina is the passage through which the baby is born

More Facts

- When a baby girl is born, her two ovaries already contain more than one million immature eggs, some of which will be released after she reaches puberty.

- In adult men the testes produce around 250 million sperm each day. If they are not released, sperm are broken down and recycled.

- Only a few hundred sperm survive the journey to the fallopian tube.

- The uterus normally resembles an upside-down pear. But during pregnancy, as a fetus grows, the uterus expands massively to the size of a basketball, returning to its original size after birth.

Inside a uterus

Can doctors "see" a growing baby?

An ultrasound scan provides a safe way to "see" a fetus growing inside its mother's uterus. High-frequency sound waves beamed into the uterus create echoes that are turned into images by a computer. The scan shows if the fetus is developing normally and can also show whether it is a girl or a boy. This 3-D ultrasound scan also shows the umbilical cord (center) that carries blood to and from the fetus.

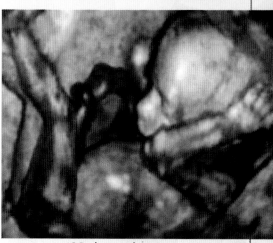

3-D ultrasound scan

What are genes?

A set of 23 chromosomes contains the instructions, called genes, required to build and run cells and, therefore, the human body. Every chromosome carries many genes. Each gene consists of a short section of the long, coiled DNA molecule that makes up the chromosome. A gene's DNA holds the coded information needed to make one of the many proteins that make your body work.

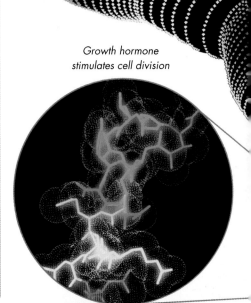

Computer model of a chromosome

Growth hormone stimulates cell division

How are identical twins the same?

The nucleus of every body cell contains structures called chromosomes that are made from DNA. This master molecule holds the instructions that make you look human but also give you individual features that make you stand out from the crowd. You inherit DNA from both your parents. When humans reproduce, slightly different DNA instructions from each parent come together in the fertilized egg to create a unique individual. Occasionally, a fertilized egg splits into two separate cells. These develop into twin babies that look identical because they share exactly the same DNA.

How many chromosomes do I have?

There are 23 pairs of chromosomes inside a body cell, which are here arranged and numbered in order of size from 1 (longest) to 22 (shortest). The 23rd pair is the sex chromosomes —XY in males and XX in females —which determine a person's sex. One member of each chromosome pair comes from your mother and one from your father. When a man's sperm and a woman's egg fuse at fertilization, each contributes 23 chromosomes, making 46 chromosomes in the fertilized egg that develops into a baby.

Human chromosomes

| 1 | 2 | 3 | 4 | 5 | 6 |

| 7 | 8 | 9 | 10 | 11 | 12 |

| 13 | 14 | 15 | 16 | 17 | 18 |

XY chromosomes found in males

XX chromosomes found in females

| 19 | 20 | 21 | 22 | X Y | X |

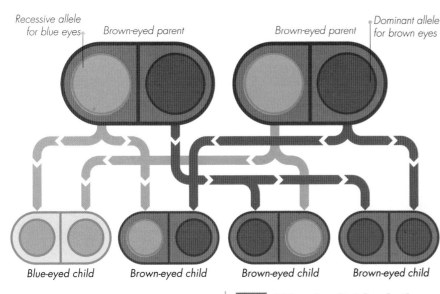

Recessive allele for blue eyes • Brown-eyed parent   Brown-eyed parent   Dominant allele for brown eyes

Blue-eyed child   Brown-eyed child   Brown-eyed child   Brown-eyed child

A tongue roller

Q / A Why can some people roll their tongue?

Most of your features are each controlled by several genes. But a few depend on a single gene, including being able—or not—to roll your tongue like this. If you inherit the dominant tongue-rolling allele (version) of the gene from one or both parents, you can roll your tongue. But if you inherit the non-tongue-rolling allele from both parents, you can't.

• Different genes shown as colored bands

Q / A Why don't I look the same as my parents?

Both chromosomes—one from each parent—in a pair contain the same genes, although one of the chromosomes in the pair may carry different versions, or alleles, of those genes. While one allele (dominant) will always have an effect on the person's makeup, the other one (recessive) won't unless it is present on both chromosomes. That's why you could have blue eyes when both of your parents have brown eyes.

Reading the genome

Q / A What was the Human Genome Project?

The human genome is all the DNA contained in one set of 23 chromosomes. During the Human Genome Project (1990–2003), scientists around the world discovered the sequence of the "letters" in DNA molecules that make up the "words" of the instructions (genes) that control our cells. They did this by breaking up DNA molecules in order to "read" the "letters" in order. This also allowed them to locate the position of genes on chromosomes.

More Facts

■ It was once believed that there were 100,000 genes in the human genome. The Human Genome Project suggests that there are only 20,000–25,000.

■ Stretched out, the DNA in the chromosomes of one tiny cell would extend more than 6.5 ft (2 m). All the DNA in your body would extend across 124 billion miles (200,000,000,000 km).

■ If you can't see an eye shape here, you are probably colorblind, meaning that you can't distinguish certain colors. This is caused by a gene carried on the X sex chromosome. Boys have just one X chromosome, so if they inherit the gene, they are colorblind. But to become colorblind, girls have to inherit the gene on both of their X chromosomes, which is why it's much rarer in girls.

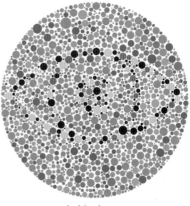

Colorblindness test

When a baby is born, its brain contains the adult complement of 100 billion neurons (nerve cells), but it is just one quarter of the size of an adult's. That is because those neurons have few interconnections and have yet to link up to form the massive network that makes us so smart. Gaps between the skull bones that surround a child's brain allow the brain to expand as the network grows.

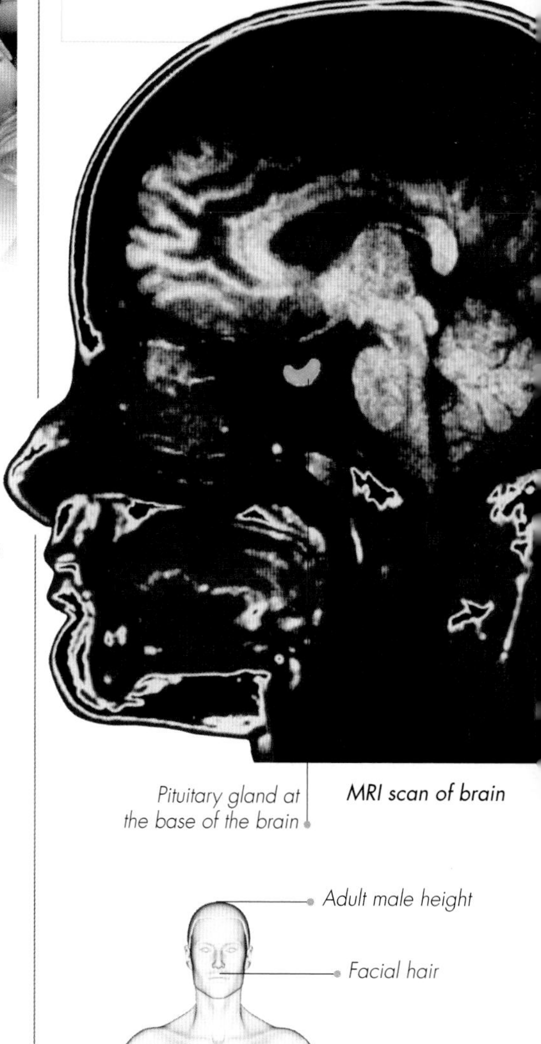

Why is my body changing?

As we get older, each of us follows the same sequence of changes. Our bones grow as we do, and our brains become increasingly more complex as we experience the world around us. But possibly the most dramatic change is during puberty, when children become young adults. Puberty starts in late childhood, earlier in girls than in boys. During puberty, both girls and boys get taller, their body shapes change, and their reproductive systems "turn on" and start working; girls start having their period and release eggs, while boys start making sperm.

Pituitary gland at the base of the brain

MRI scan of brain

Q A What happens to a teenager's body?

Both girls and boys show a growth spurt at the same time as their body shapes change to resemble an adult woman or an adult man. A girl's body becomes more rounded, and she develops breasts, while a boy's body becomes more muscular. Both sexes grow hair in their armpits and around their genitals.

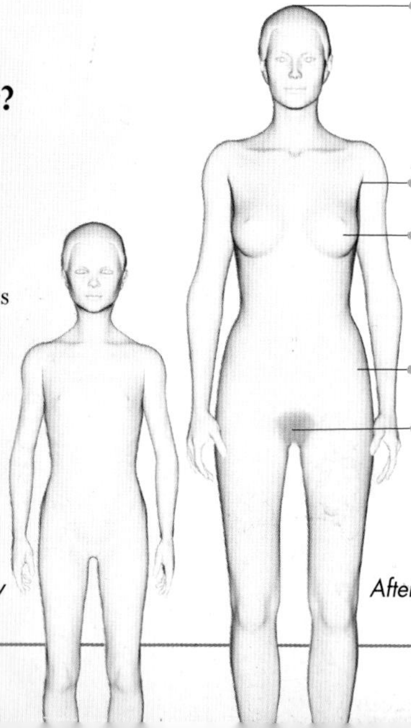

Adult female height

Armpit hair

Breast development

Before puberty

Broadened hips

Pubic hair

Adult male height

Facial hair

Broadened chest

Pubic hair

Enlarged genitals

More muscular body

Before puberty

After puberty

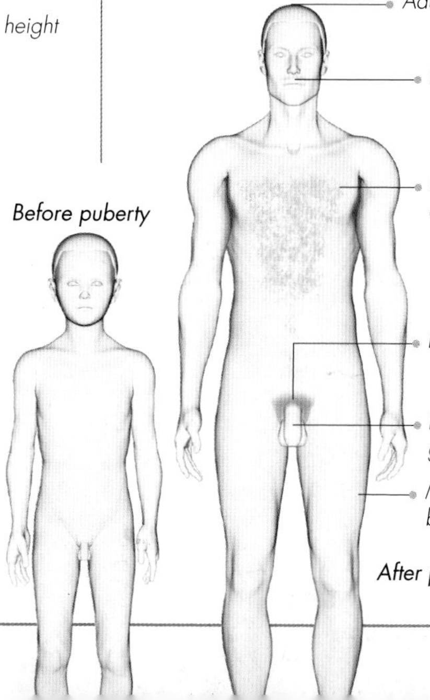

After puberty

1 Brain neurons (green) have few links between them. Membranes span the gaps between skull bones that allow the brain to expand.

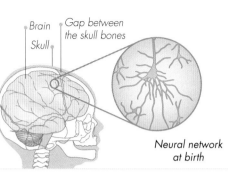

Brain

Skull

Gap between the skull bones

Neural network at birth

2 As a result of learning and experience, connections between neurons greatly increase, making the brain almost adult sized.

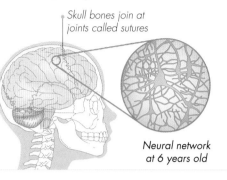

Skull bones join at joints called sutures

Neural network at 6 years old

3 The full-sized brain has a complete neural network, and immovable sutures lock the skull bones together.

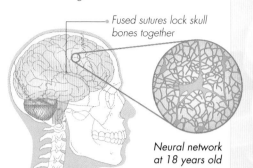

Fused sutures lock skull bones together

Neural network at 18 years old

Q A Why does puberty start?

The events of puberty are initially started by two hormones released from the pituitary gland. In girls these hormones target the ovaries, causing the release of eggs and female sex hormones. In males they target the genitals, causing the release of male sex hormones and stimulating sperm production. It is the sex hormones that trigger the changes in girls' and boys' bodies.

Egg (red) released from an ovary

More Facts

- In girls puberty generally begins between the ages of 10 and 12, while in boys it is between 12 and 14.

- Adolescence is the word that describes all the changes to a person, including puberty and changes in behavior, that are completed by the late teens.

- Special sweat glands in the armpits only start working at puberty. They release a thicker sweat that, when broken down by bacteria, produces body odor.

Sweat on skin

Q A What is the menstrual cycle?

This sequence of events, which repeats itself every 28 days, on average, prepares the uterus to receive a fertilized egg. During a menstrual cycle, the lining of the uterus thickens, and around day 14, an egg is released from an ovary. If the egg is fertilized, it implants in the thick uterus lining. If not, the lining is shed during a period.

Hand of a 1-year-old

Q A How do bones get bigger?

The skeleton forms as a baby grows in the uterus. At first the skeleton is made of flexible cartilage, but gradually this is replaced by harder bone. This process, called ossification, continues into the teenage years, as shown by these two x-rays. In the one-year-old's hand, many "bones" are still largely cartilage—which continues to grow in length. In the 20-year-old's hand, growth and ossification are complete.

Hand of a 20-year-old

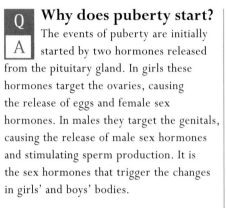

Why don't we live forever?

Aging and death are natural parts of the human life cycle that is "programmed" into our cells. By the time we reach our 60s, the first signs of wear and tear appear. The skin wrinkles, hair thins and whitens, eyesight and hearing can get worse, thinking slows down, and we get more aches and pains. But many changes can be kept at bay by a good diet and by regular exercise such as the gentle movements of tai chi.

Q A What makes our body age?

Our cells, and their instruction-carrying chromosomes, regularly divide in order to repair and maintain our bodies. But the number of times they can divide in a lifetime is limited. Chromosomes have protective tips called telomeres, which get shorter with every division. When they eventually disappear, cell division is no longer possible, which leads to signs of aging.

Telomeres cap the ends of a chromosome

Chromosome is one of 46 inside every cell

Chromosome

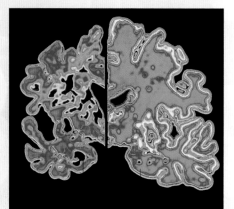

Brain cross section with Alzheimer's

Healthy brain cross section

Q A Does everyone lose their memory as they get older?

It isn't inevitable. Although the loss of nerve cells in old age usually make thinking and reaction times slower and memory less efficient, keeping the mind active helps reverse these changes. But people who develop dementia—the most common form of which is Alzheimer's disease—suffer dramatic brain shrinkage, causing memory loss and confusion that are not reversible.

What makes our skin wrinkly?

One of the most visible signs of aging is wrinkled skin. Young skin is kept strong and stretchy by fibers of collagen and elastin. With age, though, skin gets thinner, produces less protective oil, and the number of collagen and elastin fibers in it decrease. That's why older skin is looser and more wrinkly.

Jeanne Calment (1875–1997)—the oldest person ever

Replacement hand with moving parts

Why do older people's bones break more easily?

Throughout life our bones constantly reshape by breaking down and rebuilding themselves. As we age, bone breaks itself down faster than it can be replaced. This makes bones less dense and weaker so that they fracture more easily. Loss of bone density is the most dramatic in osteoporosis, a condition found mainly in older women. In addition, joints between bones tend to get stiffer with age.

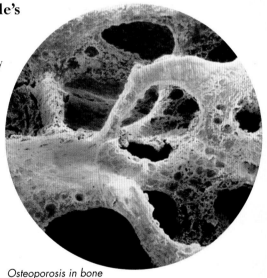

Osteoporosis in bone

Can we replace body parts?

If we lose a hand, leg, or other body part, either through a disease or an accident, it will not grow back. But it can probably be replaced. This bionic hand, for example, is "wired up" so that the fingers move as instructed by its owner's brain. This enables it to grip a pen just like a normal hand. Internal organs, such as kidneys or the heart, that have been damaged or are diseased can be replaced by healthy organs provided by donors.

Artificial skin

More Facts

- Most of us will live for much longer than our ancestors because we have better diets, live in cleaner, healthier surroundings, and receive superior medical care.

- On average, women live longer than men. Life expectancy in the Western world is about 83 for women and 78 for men.

- Men can produce sperm for a lifetime, but women stop releasing eggs at the time of menopause, which occurs, on average, at the age of 51.

- Skin that is damaged may soon be able to be replaced by artificial skin grown in a laboratory. It would be made with a patient's own cells so that it is not rejected by the patient's body.

INDEX

CREDITS

Dorling Kindersley would like to thank Caitlin Doyle for proof-reading and Americanization, and Jackie Brind for the index.

The publisher would like to thank the following for their kind permission to reproduce their photographs:
(Key: a-above; b-below/bottom; c-center; l-left; r-right; t-top)

2-3 Corbis: Photo Quest Ltd / Science Photo Library. 4 Corbis: Steve Gschmeissner / Science Photo Library (bl); Visuals Unlimited (cl) (tl). 4-7 Corbis: Visuals Unlimited (background). 5 Corbis: Steve Allen / Brand X (cr); Visuals Unlimited (br). Getty Images: Spike Walker (tr). 6 Corbis: Kurt Kormann (cl); Photo Quest Ltd / Science Photo Library (tl). Getty Images: Sandra Baker (bl). 7 Corbis: Visuals Unlimited (tc). Getty Images: Steve Gschmeissner / Science Photo Library (bl); Dr. Kessel & Dr. Kardon / Tissues & Organs (br). 8-9 Science Photo Library: Steve Gschmeissner. 10 Science Photo Library: Simon Fraser (cr). 10-19 Corbis: Visuals Unlimited (background). 11 Science Photo Library: (br); A. Dowsett, Health Protection Agency (c); Prof. P. Motta / Dept. Of Anatomy / University "La Sapienza", Rome (tl). 12 Science Photo Library: Dr Jeremy Burgess (cl); L'oreal / Eurelios (tl). 13 Science Photo Library: Steve Gschmeissner (tl) (cr). 15 Science Photo Library: Dept. Of Clinical Radiology, Salisbury District Hospital (cr); Andrew Syred (tc). 16 Science Photo Library: Don Fawcett (bc). 17 Corbis: (cr). Getty Images: Mike Kemp (cl). 18 Corbis: Wally McNamee (c). 19 Corbis: Dan McCoy - Rainbow/

Science Faction (bc). Science Photo Library: DU Cane Medical Imaging Ltd (cr); Zephyr (br). 20-21 Corbis: Dennis Kunkel Microscopy, Inc./ Visuals Unlimited (c). 22 Corbis: Dimitri Lundt/ TempSport (cl). 22-29 Corbis: Visuals Unlimited (background). 23 Corbis: Image Source (cr). Science Photo Library: Dr Tony Brain (bl). 24 Corbis: MedicalRF.com (cra); Science Photo Library/ Photo Quest Ltd (cl) (cr). 24-25 Getty Images: 3D4Medical.com. 25 Corbis: Dennis Kunkel Microscopy, Inc./ Visuals Unlimited (bc); Reuters (cr). Science Photo Library: BSIP GEMS / Europe (tc). 26 Corbis: Oliver Rossi (tl). Getty Images: Nucleus Medical Art, Inc. (bl). 27 Getty Images: Jupiterimages (c). Science Photo Library: Dr Gary Settles (tc); Eye Of Science (cl). 28 Corbis: Visuals Unlimited (c). Science Photo Library: (bl) (bc). 29 Corbis: Mod Art / CSA Images (tc); Roy Hsu/ Blend Images (br). 30-31 Getty Images: Thomas Deerinck. 32-39 Corbis: Visuals Unlimited (background). 33 Alamy Images: Chuck Franklin (tc). Getty Images: Iconica / Brick House Pictures (bc). National Geographic Stock: Cary Wolinsky (cr). Science Photo Library: Steve Gschmeissner (clb); C. J. Guerin, PHD, MRC Toxicology Unit (cl). 34 Science Photo Library: Omikron (bl). 35 Getty Images: Fabrice Coffrini / AFP (bc). 36 Science Photo Library: Steve Gschmeissner (bc). 37 Corbis: Wally McNamee (cr). Getty Images: Digital Vision / James Woodson (c); Workbook Stock / Thierry Grun (bc). Science Photo Library: Susumu Nishinaga (cl). 38 Science Photo Library: (bl). 39 Corbis: Amanaimages (bc). Getty Images: Iconica / Jeffrey Coolidge (tr); StockFood Creative / Ian Garlick (cr). Science Photo Library: Steve Gschmeissner (c). 40-41 Corbis: Visuals Unlimited. 42 Science Photo Library: Steve Gschmeissner (br). 43 Science Photo Library: NIBSC (tl); Antonia Reeve (tr). 44 Getty Images: Visuals Unlimited / Dr. Fred Hossler (c).

45 Getty Images: Jasper Juinen (br). Science Photo Library: CNRI (cr) (crb); Susumu Nishinaga (c). 47 Alamy Images: Hugh Threlfall (br). Corbis: Frans Lanting (cr). Science Photo Library: Eye Of Science (tc); Roger Harris (c). 48 Science Photo Library: Pasieka (cra). 48-49 Science Photo Library: Eye Of Science (bc); NIBSC (tc). 49 Getty Images: Stockbyte (cb). Science Photo Library: David Goodsell (br); Steve Gschmeissner (cr); Dr Gopal Murti (tr). 50-51 Science Photo Library: Steve Gschmeissner. 52-59 Corbis: Visuals Unlimited (background). 53 Corbis: Visuals Unlimited (crb). Science Photo Library: GE Medical Systems (br). 54 Corbis: Tim Pannell (tl). Science Photo Library: CNRI (br/XY); Dept. Of Clinical Cytogenetics, Addenbrookes Hospital (br); Pasieka (cr). 54-55 Science Photo Library: Pasieka. 55 Corbis: Andrew Brookes (cr). Science Photo Library: David Nicholls (br). 56 Corbis: Randy Faris (tl). Science Photo Library: Scott Camazine (cr). 57 Science Photo Library: (br); Professors P.M. Motta & J. Van Blerkom (c); Richard Wehr / Custom Medical Stock Photo (bl). 58 Getty Images: Mike Kemp (cr). Science Photo Library: Pasieka (bl) (c). 59 Corbis: EPA / Waltraud Grubitzsch (tr); Pascal Parrot (tl). Science Photo Library: Mauro Fermariello (br); Prof. P. Motta / Dept. Of Anatomy / University "La Sapienza", Rome (c). 60-61 Corbis: Visuals Unlimited. 62-63 Corbis: Photo Quest Ltd/ Science Photo Library

Jacket images: Front: Science Photo Library: Susumu Nishinaga (background); Pasieka c (skull). Back: Corbis: Jens Nieth bl; Visuals Unlimited cla; Science Photo Library: Mehau Kulyk cl; Bill Longcore tl; Susumu Nishinaga clb

All other images © Dorling Kindersley
For further information see: www.dkimages.com

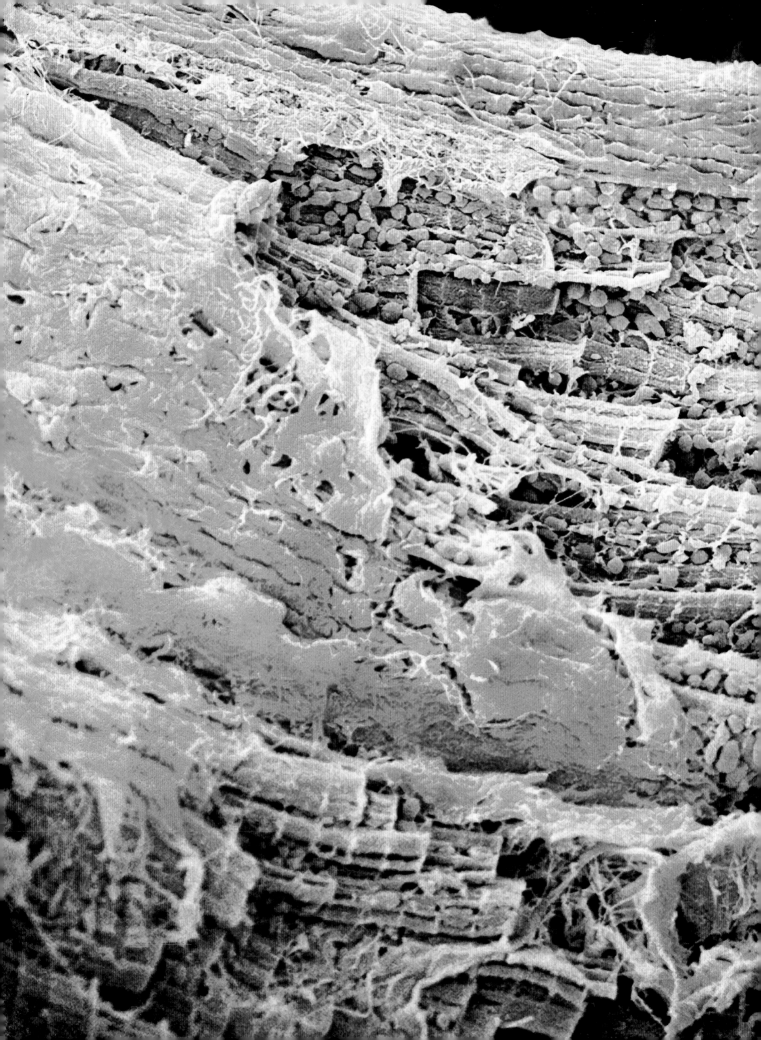